THE BLACK AMERICAN IN SOCIOLOGICAL THOUGHT

The Black American in Sociological Thought

New Perspectives on Black America

General Editor: Herbert Hill

by Stanford M. Lyman

CAPRICORN BOOKS: *New York*

CAPRICORN BOOKS EDITION, 1973

Copyright © 1972 by Stanford M. Lyman

SBN: 399-10928-5

Library of Congress Catalog Card Number: 77-181407

Printed in the United States of America

To the memory of
Horace R. Cayton

Acknowledgments

THIS BOOK has its earliest origins in my boyhood days and nights spent working in my father's grocery store in the heart of San Francisco's black ghetto. The federal bulldozer has long since leveled the store and left the street in a new form, but the memories of people and events cannot be so readily eradicated. My sociological perspective has been molded by these experiences of childhood and youth, and the anonymous blacks who educated me by their own example deserve much more credit than they will ever receive.

Herbert Blumer introduced me to sociology in 1951, and I have profited from his teachings throughout my career. The theoretical outlook that informs this work arose out of my studies with Kenneth E. Bock. His own essays on historical processes and the theory of social change have laid the foundation for a new sociology released from the burdensome errors of evolutionism and ahistoricism. Hopefully this book will advance that sociology one more step.

Over the years I have benefited from discussions on race relations and sociological theory with Kingsley Davis, Reinhard Bendix, Nathan Glazer, William Kornhauser, William Petersen, Philip Selznick, and Tamotsu Shibutani. I am particularly indebted to the encouragement toward historical sociology given by Wolfram Eberhard and H. Franz Schurmann.

The idea for this book was first suggested to me by

Herbert Hill. His own studies on the history of the black worker are an outstanding contribution, as well as an inspiration to further research. He took time from his busy schedule as writer, teacher, and labor director of the National Association for the Advancement of Colored People to discuss each chapter with me and to aid in countless ways in the preparation for publication.

My colleagues at the University of Nevada gave much guidance and encouragement to my research. I am especially grateful for the advice and suggestions of David Harvey. The manuscript was discussed with and various chapters were read by Carl Backman, James Richardson and Lyle T. Warner. I am also grateful for the patient criticism of two graduate students, John Scott Fuller and Tetsuden Kashima. The students in my course "Race and Ethnic Relations" helped by their comments and responses to my lectures on race theory in American sociology.

Throughout the research and writing I was aided and criticized by my colleague in so many other endeavors, Marvin B. Scott. He read each chapter, made many editorial and substantive suggestions, and provided friendship, encouragement, and moral support. His wife, Joyce, also helped edit the manuscript, and provided excellent gastronomic support to my work as well.

My criticism of the work of Robert E. Park and his colleagues at Chicago was aided immeasurably by Horace R. Cayton. On many evenings he listened to my readings of the early drafts of the chapter on Park. Always loyal to his mentors at Chicago, Cayton did not shrink from helping in an intellectual critique of their work. Moreover, he provided personal anecdotes, letters, and documents which further informed the study. His untimely death before the manuscript appeared in published form is a matter of deep regret. I have dedicated this book to him as a small memento of his great contribution to American letters and black life.

Portions of this manuscript have appeared in different form in journals and convention papers. "The Race Relations Cycle of Robert E. Park," a preliminary formulation of the much longer chapter that appears here, was the invitational paper presented at the annual meeting of the Pacific Sociological Association at Long Beach, California, in 1967 and later published in *Pacific Sociological Review* (Vol. 11, No. 1, Spring, 1968). I am grateful to C. Wilson Record for the invitation and to Donald Ball, Horace R. Cayton, Nathan Glazer, William Petersen, and Marvin B. Scott for helpful criticism of that paper. The final chapter of this book was presented in a preliminary draft at the annual meetings of the Ohio Valley Sociological Association in 1970 under the title "Toward a Sociology of the Negro: An Ethnomethodological Approach." Donald Ball very kindly arranged for this presentation. An abridged form of the chapter on Gordon Allport was given at the annual meeting of the Society for the Study of Social Problems in Washington, D.C., in 1970. I appreciate the invitation extended by Jack Douglas.

Eileen Coughlin helped edit the manuscript for publication. Mrs. Helen Cross supervised the typing of the manuscript. Mrs. Sonny Minidew typed the early drafts. Their work is much appreciated.

For all errors and misinterpretations I accept complete responsibility.

La Jolla, California
December 20, 1970

Stanford M. Lyman

Contents

THE BLACK AMERICAN IN SOCIOLOGICAL THOUGHT

I

SOCIAL DARWINISM AND THE SOCIOLOGICAL STUDY OF THE BLACK AMERICAN

THE Civil War was fought to resolve the issue of the place of blacks in American society. The issue was only partly settled on the battlefield of Appomattox; it was introduced anew a hundred years later on the battlefield of Watts. Between these two encounters, a more quiescent conflict was carried on in sociological literature: No subject so captivated American sociology as the black man.

To trace the black man in American sociology is tantamount to tracing the history of American sociology itself. Concern with blacks spawned, in the writings of Henry Hughes and George Fitzhugh, the first sociology texts.[1] It was a focal issue in the early Social Darwinist perspectives of Lester Frank Ward and William Graham Sumner.[2] It was the testing ground for the theories of intimacy and feeling of William I. Thomas[3] and Charles Horton Cooley.[4] It was one strand of the inspiration for a whole new sociology—to be known as the Chicago School—forged in the hands of Robert Park[5] and Louis Wirth. It was the dilemma that brought to our shores the great Swedish social scientist Gunnar Myrdal.[6] It was, along with the issue of anti-Semitism, the stimulus for intensive investigations into the psychology of racial prejudice, culminating in the widely influential study by T. W. Adorno and his associates.[7] Despite a hundred years of effort, however, the black man continues to elude sociological explanation.

From 1815 to 1859 the "American School" of ethnology developed the theory of "polygenism," in which it was held that the races of men are in fact separate species. Although the motives of these ethnologists were for the most part scientific and were intended to refute prevailing theological doctrines, their conception of the origins of races lent support to slavery and reinforced prejudice against blacks.[8] The first two sociological treatises produced in America—Henry Hughes' *Treatise on Sociology, Theoretical and Practical* and George Fitzhugh's *Sociology for the South: Or, the Failure of Free Society*— were tracts written in defense of slavery. Hughes argued that slavery was "morally and civilly good"[9] and hence should be preserved; Fitzhugh held that only in a society built upon Christianity and slavery (and eschewing liberty, equality, and laissez-faire ideals) could morality and order be maintained.[10]

By 1880 a new perspective came to dominate sociological inquiry. This was Social Darwinism,[11] which found its most profound expression in the writings of Lester Frank Ward and William Graham Sumner. Their highly stimulating discussions of man's control (or the lack of it) over social forces created such controversy over race-relations theory and practice that the debate continues today. Ward and Sumner spent a considerable portion of their intellectual energies debating about the relationship of man to the forces governing historical and social change. Two schools seemed to emerge: a conservative and deterministic one led by Sumner, and a liberal, less deterministic one led by Ward.

Sumner emphasized the conservative role of folkways and mores in society,[12] introduced the idea of cultural relativism, and opposed the "absurd effort" of philosophers and reformers to "make the world over."[13] He explained the racial troubles of America as arising out of the breakup of the harmonious relations that had existed between blacks and whites prior to the abolition of slavery:

In our southern states, before the civil war, whites and blacks had formed habits of action and feeling towards each other. They lived in peace and concord, and each one grew up in the ways which were traditional and customary. The civil war abolished legal rights and left the two races to learn how to live together under other relations than before. The whites have never been converted from the old mores. Those who still survive look back with regret and affection to the old social usages and customary sentiments and feelings. The two races have not yet made new mores. Vain attempts have been made to control the new order by legislation. The only result is the proof that legislation cannot make mores.[14]

For Sumner the future of race relations is unpredictable and problematic, but about one thing he was sure: Whatever that future is, it will be consistent with the mores of the peoples involved and it will not be subject to the activities of idealists and ethical reformers.

It is only just now [Sumner wrote] that the new society seems to be taking shape. There is a trend in the mores now as they begin to form under the new state of things. It is not at all what the humanitarians hoped and expected. The two races are separating more than ever before. The strongest point in the new code seems to be that any white man is boycotted and despised if he "associates with Negroes." Some are anxious to interfere and try to control. They take their stand on ethical views of what is going on. It is evidently impossible for anyone to interfere. We are like spectators at a great convulsion. The results will be such as the facts and forces call for. We cannot foresee them . . . the mores which once were are a memory. Those which anyone thinks ought to be are a dream. The only thing with which we can deal are those which are.[15]

For Ward, on the other hand, man is not a mere spectator at the drama of social evolution. Rather, he is an actor on the scene whose thoughts and deeds (or whose errors and failures to act) constitute crucial elements in the action and thus modify the evolutionary process.

Through his doctrine of "social telesis"[16] Ward opposed the conservative doctrines of Herbert Spencer and attacked Sumner's position that the state should not interfere with social development. Although Ward subscribed to the theory that the genesis of the state was to be found in the struggle between races—a theory developed in Europe by Ludwig Gumplowicz[17] and Gustav Ratzenhofer[18]—he believed that this early struggle, resulting in caste relations and slavery, was only the first of a series of stages leading to the emergence of the societal state. A final stage of homogeneous nationhood could not arise until after stages describing the development of free labor, industrial systems, landed property, a priesthood, a leisure class, government by law, the idea of the state, political liberty, property, a business class, and the sense of peoplehood had preceded it.[19]

Ward objected to the prevailing thesis that behavioral differences in races are hereditary, that the races have separate origins, and that race mixture would bring about retrogression. Hence he challenged the idea that one race is "older" than another, that the "lower races" cannot achieve the same material and intellectual developments found in the Occident, and that the social setting does not have a significant effect on racial change and progress:

It is not therefore proved that intellectual equality, which can be safely predicated of all classes in the white race, in the yellow race, or in the black race, each taken by itself, cannot also be predicated of all races taken together, and it is still more clear that there is no race and no class of human beings who are incapable of assimilating the social achievement of mankind and of profitably employing the social heritage.[20]

In his conception of the future of mankind, Ward projected an evolution in which races would be abolished and all humankind would be undifferentiated by hereditary marks. "If we could but peer far enough into the great future," he wrote, "we should see this planet of ours ultimately peopled with a single homogeneous and completely assimilated race of men—the human race—in the composition of which could be detected all the great commanding qualities of every one of its racial components."[21] Following this view, Ward argued that a true society must be founded on equality: "A class of individuals possessing wealth, intelligence, or lineage, cannot be called society. It is not even an aristocracy, it is an oligarchy. It only increases the number of rulers, and thereby increases the burdens of people. Neither can it be called society when, where distinct races occupy the same territory, one race excludes all others, or when any race or class is excluded."[22]

Thus Ward and Sumner, though in profound disagreement with respect to man's control over the social forces, did agree that the basis of behavior is cultural and social rather than hereditary.

With William I. Thomas a new emphasis emerges in the study of race relations. Although he tended to assert that racial prejudice is somehow innate, he differentiated it from a caste orientation and skin prejudice. "When not complicated with caste-feeling, race prejudice is, after all, very impermanent, of no more stability, perhaps, than fashions."[23] Thomas saw the situation of the black in the United States as varying according to locale:

Of the relation of black to white in this country it is perhaps true that the antipathy of the southerner for the Negro is rather caste-feeling than race prejudice, while the feeling of the notherner is race prejudice proper. In the North, where there has been no contact with the Negro and no activity connections, there is no caste-feeling, but there exists a sort of *skin*-prejudice—a horror of the external aspect of the Negro—and many northerners report that they have a feeling against cating from a dish handled by a Negro. The association of master and slave in the South was, however, close, even if not intimate, and much of the feeling of physical repulsion for a black skin disappeared. . . . But while color was not here repulsive, it was so ineradicably associated with inferiority that it was impossible for a southern white to think the Negro into his own class.[24]

If Thomas believed that racial prejudice might be reduced by sympathetic relationships and intimate association between the races,[25] Charles Horton Cooley emphasized the inevitability of castelike relationships developing in biracial societies:

Two races of different temperament and capacity, distinct to the eye and living side by side in the same community, tend strongly to become castes, no matter how equal the social system may otherwise be. . . . The race caste existing in the Southern United States illustrates the impotence of democratic traditions to overcome the caste spirit when fostered by obvious physical and psychical differences. This spirit is immeasurably strong on the part of the whites, and there is no apparent prospect of its diminution.[26]

Cooley believed that racial differences are rooted in the biological nature of man, but, like Sumner and Ward, he doubted the validity of genetic explanations alone:

> Of such a hereditary division we have almost no definite knowledge, except as regards the somewhat superficial traits of color and physiognomy. It is even possible to doubt whether there is any important innate physical difference among the several branches of mankind. It is certain that different spirits are to be found in different races. . . . In other words, a group soul, a special *ethos* or *mores* is the sure result of historical causes acting for centuries in a social system; so that different souls will exist whether the race is different or not. And as race differences, when present, are always accompanied by historical differences, it is not possible to make out just how much is due to them alone.[27]

Cooley proposed that the American government continue to restrict Oriental immigration and that China and Japan likewise forbid the settlement of whites in order to "avoid the rise of an unnecessary caste problem."[28] With respect to blacks, Cooley seemed to feel that they would forever remain a subjugated caste and that, therefore, the enlightened whites ought to combine their despotic rule with a compassionate benevolence:

> The practical question here is not that of abolishing castes but of securing just and kindly relations between them, of reconciling the fact of caste with ideals of freedom and right. This is difficult but not evidently impossible, and a right spirit, together with a government firmly repressive of the lower passions of both races, should go far to achieve it. There seems to be no reason in the nature of things why divergent races, like

divergent individuals, should not unite in common service of the ideals to which all human nature bears allegiance—I mean ideals of kindness, fair play and so on. And the white man, in claiming superiority, assumes the chief responsibility for bringing this state of things to pass.[29]

Thomas and Cooley helped usher in a new era in American sociology—an era that found its spatial locus at the University of Chicago. At Chicago the two figures that came to dominate studies in race relations were Robert Park and Louis Wirth. Park and Wirth concentrated on the effects of race contacts, the former developing a cyclical theory of racial relations,[30] the latter carefully defining the concept of minority to refer to those racial, national and religious groups that are in some sense dominated by other groups.[31] Their work moved the study of race relations away from attempts to demonstrate superiority in racial or cultural traits and toward the study of group positions in society.

In addition to the study of how racial groups came to occupy specific social locations in society, sociologists began to look at the ways in which society assigned these positions and the images that positioned groups had of themselves and of other groups. A host of studies analyzed caste and etiquette in the Deep South, merging anthropological and psychological explanations to account for a peculiar social system.[32]

Still another comprehensive orientation was taken by Gunnar Myrdal, who stressed not only the social structure in which racial relations occur but also the nonreciprocal orientations of blacks and whites toward each other.[33] Myrdal also emphasized the disparity between the American creed of equality and the actual conduct of Americans toward blacks. He believed that this disparity created an inherently unstable dissonance and that this instability would ultimately be resolved in the triumph of egalitarianism over racism.

Gradually the emphasis on the cultural factors in race prejudice was modified by an increasing interest in the psychology of racial attitudes. Prejudice was redefined as an element of the personality, whose development is primarily a function of socialization.[34] Antipathy toward blacks, Jews, and Orientals came to be perceived as a kind of individual disorder that might be relieved by exhortation, propaganda, education, therapy, or association.[35] The most important study in this genre, *The Authoritarian Personality*,[36] discovered a personality type so rigid that it appears to require therapies far more intense than are currently available. The resistance to change in authoritarian persons appears not to warrant the optimism of those who subscribe to available ameliorative approaches.

Combining all these approaches in a new emergent formulation of system and cycle, Talcott Parsons has recently presented yet another theoretical statement that promises the integration of the black into American society, the ultimate stability of the American social system and, yet, the permanent strains and anguish of racial prejudice.

Conclusion

Despite a hundred years of academic efforts to study the black man, the curious fact emerges that of all areas of sociological inquiry the field of race relations is theoretically the least developed.[37]

To understand this curious fact we will begin our analysis with the man who is unquestionably the pivotal figure in the theory of race relations—namely, Robert Park. We will carefully examine Park's systematic formulations, especially his theory of the race-relations cycle, in the next chapter. But here some preliminary remarks may be made.

Park, in developing his race-relations cycle, adapted ideas that were already a familiar feature of Western thought, ideas that could be traced back to Aristotle's conceptions of science, politics, and social change. Ever since Aristotle argued that science could only study that which behaved in accordance with slow, orderly, continuous, and teleological movement,[38] adherents to his view have been led to make a radical separation of events from processes. The study of "natural" processes independent of historical events has produced an evolutionist anthropology, narrative history, and functionalist sociology.[39] In the case of anthropology and sociology the concentration on stages of development or cycles of change deterred any interest in the comparative and systematic study of events, from which there might have arisen a theory quite different from that postulated by evolutionist orientations.[40]

Once Park had systematically organized thought about race relations in accordance with cyclical movement, sociologists who followed after him have been forced into one of two difficult theoretical positions. Either they have insisted on a particular teleology to explain racial relations, forcing facts and events onto a Procrustean bed dictated by this teleology, or they have abandoned altogether a concern for the historical record and concentrated their attention on psychological orientations or ad hoc approaches to race issues.

There has existed in sociology for more than fifty years an anti-Aristotelian position. Represented by the work of Frederick Teggart,[41] Margaret T. Hodgen,[42] Kenneth E. Bock,[43] and Robert A. Nisbet,[44] this position attacks the very assumptions that guided Aristotle's original formulation and develops a telling critique against the derivative schools of history, anthropology, and sociology which it has spawned. Although the method of comparative study advocated by this school has not yet been applied to the sociology of race relations, it would appear to offer a fruitful departure for new theory and understanding. Furthermore, the application of the concepts and perceptions of phenomenological sociology, represented in such innovative schools of thought as ethnomethodology, should be integrated with a thoroughgoing historical sociology to produce a new and dynamic sociology of the black man.

In the following chapters—which deal with Park's race-relations cycle, John Dollard's study of caste and etiquette in the Deep South, Myrdal's conception of an American dilemma, Adorno's theory of the authoritarian personality, and Parsons' concept of a social-systems approach to race relations—I will develop a critique in the tradition of Teggart and his followers and show how any study of man and society, and, therefore, certainly the study of race relations and the black man, must have as its *sine qua non* a concern for events and happenings, for history and for its systematic analysis.

II

THE RACE-RELATIONS CYCLE OF ROBERT E. PARK

ROBERT E. PARK'S race-relations cycle is indisputably one of the most important contributions to sociological thought. However, despite widespread discussion and criticism, neither Park's philosophical assumptions nor the full potentiality of his theory has been examined completely.

In his formulation Park postulated a generalized law of racial relations that is universally applicable and at the same time descriptive of the evolution of race relations in any particular society. The theory would thus be a guide to both history and current affairs: It would explain the events of the past as well as evaluate current activities in terms of their evolutionary propriety. It is ideology too, for Park believed that once the racial cycle was completed, the social arena would be cleared of those racial impediments interfering with the inevitable class struggle. As theory and ideology, as a guide to the past and a measure of the present, Park's cycle has seen wide service in sociological theory, social reform, and practical politics.

The race-relations cycle proceeds in four stages—contact, conflict, accommodation, and assimilation—in the course of which there unfolds a great cultural and social drama. Each act of this drama is dictated by laws of history and culture, Park writes, and the sequence cannot be halted or diverted. The first stage, contact, occurs when two races meet on a "racial frontier" and are obliged to interact.

Conflict arises when the races compete for valuable resources. The conflict is resolved by accommodation, in which a stable but asymmetrical and unequal social order is established. Finally, accommodation gives way to assimilation, when the two races merge culturally and, ultimately, physically. In the end, society becomes homogeneous.

Park regarded his race-relations cycle as a law of historical development, to be treated as virtually ineluctable: "The race relations cycle . . . is apparently progressive and irreversible. Customs regulations, immigration restrictions and racial barriers may slacken the tempo of the movement; may perhaps halt it altogether for a time; but cannot change its direction; cannot at any rate reverse it."[1]

The notion that race relations follow a cycle is not original with Park. He is indebted to the evolutionary theories of Social Darwinism. And prior to that, philosophers and theologians had traditionally studied man's course through history in terms of epochs succeeding one another in some kind of definite order. Such cycles were regarded as "natural histories" and based on Aristotelian concepts.[2]

Perhaps Park's greatest, though unacknowledged, intellectual debt is to Aristotle. To Aristotle, all science, including history, is natural science, and biological change is a model for all change. Things in nature change in accordance with their immanent qualities. The change is slow, continuous, and orderly, and the outcome is dictated by properties inherent in the thing changing. Nature does not act by chance or spontaneously, Aristotle argues. Rather, that which is natural occurs "all the time or for the most part" in the same way. Nature seeks to implement its own ends; hence anything that is natural behaves for the sake of its own ends. However, Aristotle observes, some things are not natural. Mistakes occasionally occur, such as biological "monstrosities." Moreover, "accidents" can arise by chance or spontaneously and interrupt nature's plan. Accidents occur when natural actions are perverted from their natural end. This presumes an act of deliberation, Aristotle concludes, and the only agent capable of deliberation is man.

Aristotelians divide what happens in the world, then, into two categories: the natural and the accidental. But science must only concern itself with "that which is always or for the most part"—in other words, with that which is natural and thus capable of scientific examination; other things belong to the world of accidents.[3] Any occurrence in the experience of a thing in nature that cannot be associated with the true natural end for which it exists must be regarded as accidental, irrelevant for scientific description.

Extending his natural science to include politics and the study of the state, Aristotle described the state as "a creation of nature" and man as "by nature a political animal."[4] He found a demonstration of this idea in the expanding sequence of family into village and then into community and ultimately into state. This developmental sequence of events occurs when nothing interferes or if there is no impediment in the natural history of a state.

But Aristotle's natural history runs afoul of the historical record.

If asked which state is described in the above natural history, an Aristotelian would answer that it must be all or most states. If it is pointed out that some states have not formed this way, the rejoinder is that these states are unnatural, they are "monstrosities."[5] Natural history, then, is a science of the normal based on the definition of "normal" as that which occurs if nothing interferes; hence what is normal cannot be derived from the historical record.

Aristotle had in mind what later men would refer to as an "organism" when he defined things which carry within themselves their source or principle of change, which pass through an orderly sequence of metamorphoses, which change in order to realize an inherent potential, and which finally fall into decay or come to rest. In this light, social institutions can be studied as organisms. Their origins can be looked at to discover their potential—*i.e.*, why they exist; their natural history can be deduced. Moreover, considered as organisms, social institutions can become "diseased," and "accidents" can interfere with their natural growth. From a melioristic point of view, such diseases and accidents must be treated or removed so that nature can pursue its course unmolested.

The net effect of Aristotle's theory of change has been to deter interest in the actual historical record. From a welter of happenings an Aristotelian will winnow the "natural" elements and dismiss the rest as accidents. Moreover, the Aristotelian sees all natural objects as under the control of "forces" that push them inexorably through their stages of development to their predetermined end. Because these forces are metahistorical, he concludes, they cannot be obtained from the study of events themselves. And so, it follows, they are not amenable to social action.

All the principles of Aristotle's theory of change are reproduced in Park's race-relations cycle. For example, Park insisted that race relations invariably pass through four specific stages and that one need only calculate where a given race is in the cycle to know what its past was and what its future will be.

Illustrating this point with contemporary examples, a disciple of Park might ask: Had the Chinese and whites engaged in race riots and mob violence? Then, he would answer, this only meant that the stage of conflict was in progress; it would eventually cycle into another kind of *modus vivendi*, the accommodation stage. Were the Japanese on the West Coast living in harmony with their white neighbors, peaceably pursuing trade and business? Then this was accommodation, and the subtleties and inevitable intimacies of this stage would eventually lead to assimilation. Were blacks demanding social equality with whites only to be refused at every turn? Then their demands must be out of kilter with the times. They were simply unaware that they were living in an age of accommodation and that social equality was reserved for the next stage of their relations with whites.

Park never carried out a full-scale study of ethnic groups to attempt to fit his model to reality, but he did, in 1926, lead a team of researchers in a major survey of Oriental groups on the Pacific Coast. Here, over and over, the data seemed to contradict Park's theory and suggested that just because a racial group adopts the larger society's culture, that does not necessarily guarantee its acceptance by that society. For example, two Japanese rural communities were found to be in a precarious peace with white farmers and businessmen, but one of the communities was torn asunder by hostilities among its own members.[6] San Francisco's Chinatown ghetto exhibited a full panoply of complex organization and conflict which showed no signs of disintegrating.[7] American-born Chinese and Japanese had adopted much of the culture, language, dress, habits, and opinions of conventional American society and were less frequently the victims of assaults and race riots, but considerable discrimination and social distance still separated them from white America.[8]

However, contradiction of his theory was not what Park saw in these reports. On the Pacific Coast he thought he saw the dynamics of his race cycle in action. Everywhere competition was giving way to accommodation, he said, and soon assimilation would set in. Where the evidence contradicted these observations, Park and his associates disposed of the problem by introducing Aristotle's doctrine of accidents: The race cycle was being interfered with by obstacles. Park named physical traits and the failure to establish interracial friendships as the chief obstacles to the working out of the cycle. Accidents of geography and size and composition of the minority group were also cited as interferences.

An illustration of the doctrine of accidents is found in the study of the Japanese minority in California. This study was carried out in 1926 by Winifred Raushenbush, a researcher who worked under the general supervision of Robert E. Park at the time of his race-relations survey of the Pacific Coast. According to Miss Raushenbush, the race-relations cycle was not being fulfilled for the Japanese in the town of Florin, California, because of several coincidental accidents of geography and social policy. Perhaps the most onerous impediment to assimilation, Miss Raushenbush asserted, is the fact that Florin is located near Sacramento, the seat of California's anti-Oriental movement, and, because of that, race prejudice is so rampant that social acceptance of the Japanese is extremely unlikely. Moreover, what Miss Raushenbush considers an "ignorant tactlessness" in American racial etiquette has exacerbated the race question by permitting Florin's Japanese to become the majority element in the town's population. "It should be the first rule in the book of etiquette on race relations," Miss Raushenbush wrote, "that the foreigner should never become the major element in the population unless he is a slave; in fact unless the foreigner remains a very small element in the population there is inevitable friction and alarm."[9] In her study of the Japanese in the town of Livingston, California, however, Miss Raushenbush found a more suitable "laboratory experiment in race relations"—that is, a setting in which the race cycle is being gradually fulfilled unimpeded by accidents. In Livingston the Japanese were farther away from urban anti-Orientalism. They remained a minority in the town's population and accepted without protest the imposition of segregation in a racial ghetto and did not engage in the divisive religious quarrels which separated the Buddhist from the Protestant Japanese in Florin. Miss Raushenbush thus indicated that several kinds of accidents could temporarily halt or slow down the process of assimilation: Accidents of settlement might engender a hostile race prejudice that prevented the gradual acceptance of social equality; accidents of group size might threaten the harmony necessary for peaceful coexistence between the dominant and the yet unassimilated races; accidents of pace might lead a minority group to demand more rights than its cyclical position dictated; and accidents of intragroup hostility might impede homogeneous community development.

However, Miss Raushenbush continues, if some accidents impede assimilation, others facilitate it. She believes that "intelligence" aids in cyclical fulfillment. In answer to her own question of how "the impossible" feat of interracial harmony occurred in Livingston, she writes: "The answer, strangely enough, is through intelligence. While Florin has the usual number of families—to be found in almost any community—who are morons or less, Livingston has had the fortune, rare enough in an immigrant farming community, to have possessed several men of more than ordinary imagination and energy. Two of these are a professor of agriculture who owns one of the best almond orchards in the state, and an ex-garment worker whose family belonged to the samurai class in Japan."[10]

These two leaders keep watch over the affairs of the Japanese community, guide it in its relations with whites, and enforce a gradualist program of racial advancement. Miss Raushenbush points out that very few minority communities are fortunate enough to be led by wise and sagacious men. In their absence, she argues, prejudices are bound to be sustained and racial animosities are likely to be stirred up by impolitic minority group actions. The road to assimilation is rocky, Miss Raushenbush seems to suggest, and few are likely to pass over it without stumbling on its jagged stones.

Park's own analysis of Miss Raushenbush's study indicates how he employed the doctrine of accidents to sustain the theory of the race-relations cycle. Miss Raushenbush had not explained whether Florin's Japanese would assimilate or how the "accommodated" status of Livingston's Japanese would give way to assimilation. Indeed, the tone of her study was so pessimistic that one might readily conclude that assimilation is a most unlikely outcome even when interracial life is peaceful. Park, however, in reviewing her study, suggested that the evidence presented a picture of cyclical fulfillment. Here and there accidents delayed progress, but assimilation seemed everywhere to be inevitable for all minorities. Accommodation, the penultimate stage in the race-relations cycle, would lead to assimilation as deepening interpersonal intimacy between the races broke down stereotyped thinking. He was sure that the opportunities for interracial friendship would arise in the peaceful relations generated by the acquiescence of a minority group to temporary second-class citizenship. "Personal relations and personal friendships are the great moral solvents," he wrote. "Under their influence all distinctions of class, of caste, and even of race, are dissolved into the general flux which we sometimes call democracy."[11]

The race cycle cannot be reversed, Park insists, and apparent contradictions in its movement are just that— apparent, not real. Specific events might temporarily interfere with the cycle, but nothing can permanently hold back its linear and irreversible progress. The events which for a time thwart cyclical movement are "accidents," temporary obstacles ultimately to be dismissed as phenomena not worth scientific investigation.

Although Park remained committed to his theory of a race-relations cycle throughout his life, in his later years he began to have doubts about whether assimilation would be the only final outcome of such a cycle. At the age of seventy-three, in a review of race relations in Hawaii, Park suggested that assimilation was but one possible terminus of the cycle and that permanent minority status or a caste system were just as likely. Whatever the outcome in any particular case, Park continued, it would be one that fit the culture in which the cycle had been progressing.[12] Park's important modification of the race-relations cycle went almost unnoticed at the time. Two generations of sociologists had for the most part accepted not only the general principles of the original cycle but also its promise of an eventual racelessness in the world. The actual events that described any racial group's history were either milestones down the road to its own ultimate disappearance or, if they did not fit such a scheme, temporary roadblocks which ineluctable social processes would overcome. Park's race-relations cycle had provided the essential sociological imagination for successive generations of American scholars. Thereafter they would pursue the dream of a racially homogeneous world to be ushered in by the gradual operation of social evolution.

The Race-Relations Cycle and the Black American

In an autobiographical note found among his papers after his death, Park wrote that his interest in blacks was stirred by Booker T. Washington, with whom he had enjoyed a seven-year association at Tuskegee Institute. Park wrote, "I probably learned more about human nature and society, in the South under Booker Washington, than I had learned elsewhere in all my previous studies":

I was not . . . interested in the Negro problem as that problem is ordinarily conceived. I was interested in the Negro in the South and in the curious and intricate

system which had grown up to define his relations with
white folk. I was interested, most of all, in studying the
details of the process by which the Negro was making
and has made his slow but steady advance. I became
convinced, finally, that I was observing the historical
process by which civilization, not merely here but
elsewhere, has evolved, drawing into the circle of its
influence an ever widening circle of races and peoples.[13]

The study of the black man was to become for Park a case
study for his theory of the race-relations cycle. Completion of the cycle, he believed, was an essential prerequisite
to a worldwide evolutionary movement which would
ultimately abolish separate races altogether. Park was
convinced that race conflicts would decline in the modern
world and eventually disappear entirely, leaving in their
place the struggle between classes.[14] Blacks and whites, he
believed, are together traveling along a course of history
dictated by irrevocable laws and controlled by forces
beyond their knowledge.

Such, then, was Park's premise. But the more he studied
about blacks and tried to fit the facts to his notion of a
cycle, the more he became aware of the accidents and
obstacles that slow down the cycle or temporarily halt it
altogether. As a result, although not always labeled as
such, Park's comments on blacks constitute a veritable
table of obstacles that would hinder progress. Before that
millennial day when the races would merge, a host of
difficulties would have to be overcome.

From the beginning, Park's analysis of the black man is
complicated by his rather vague conception of assimilation
and by his belief that it has *already occurred*—during the
period when blacks were held in slavery. For Park, assimilation is not founded on like-mindedness but rather on
coordinated sentiments and habits built up over a long
period of time by people who, although they might be

quite different in outlook, are nevertheless prepared to work together amicably within the society to which they belong. In other words, it is a practical working arrangement that gives the corporate character to social groups and ensures their solidarity.[15] In characteristic fashion, Park defined assimilation by a biological analogy: "The word . . . brings with it a certain borrowed significance which it carried over from physiology where it is employed to describe the process of nutrition. By a process of nutrition, somewhat similar to the physiological one, we may conceive alien peoples to be incorporated with, and made part of, the community or state."[16]

Park actually had several conceptions of assimilation in mind at once and, although his analytical distinctions were not very precise, he conceived of it in several dimensions, including the ecological, cultural, and personal. It was with respect to these latter that Park supposed blacks to have become assimilated during their enslavement, and he found it strange when Americans spoke of the black as in any sense an alien or stranger. "He has lived here longer than most of us," Park wrote, "has interbred to a greater extent than the white man with the native Indian, and is more completely a product than anyone of European origin is likely to be of the local conditions under which he was born and bred."[17]

Park argued the assimilating influence of slavery in no uncertain terms: "Slavery has been, historically, the usual method by which peoples have been incorporated into alien groups. When a member of an alien race is adopted into the family as a servant, or as a slave, and particularly when that status is made hereditary as it was in the case of the Negro after his importation to America, assimilation follows rapidly and as a matter of course."[18] He adopted a similarly unequivocal position in the debate over whether blacks retained their African heritage in slavery:

My own impression is that the amount of African tradition which the Negro brought to the United States was very small. In fact there is every reason to believe that he left behind him almost everything but his dark complexion and his tropical temperament. It is very difficult to find in the South today anything that can be traced directly back to Africa. This does not mean that there is not a great deal of superstition, conjuring, root doctoring, and magic but these we might expect to grow up anywhere among an imaginative people living in an intellectual twilight such as exists on the isolated plantations of the southern states.[19]

Finally, Park seems to have accepted uncritically the picture of antebellum plantation life as painted by pro-slavery historians,[20] and so he assumed that the relations between master and slave—and especially between master and house servants—were amicable and intimate. Here he thought he saw the subtle operation of the assimilating process. It was during the slavery period, he wrote, "and under the influences of the associations thus established, that those intimate and friendly relations between master and slave were established which are still so unintelligible to those who have looked upon slavery as if it were, always and everywhere, something inhuman and monstrous."[21] Park furthered his point by noting how willingly the black adapted to his white master's ways:

It is difficult to conceive two races farther removed from each other in temperament and tradition than the Anglo-Saxon and the Negro, and yet the Negro in the Southern States, particularly where he was adopted into the household as a family servant, learned in a comparatively short time the manners and customs of his master's family. He very soon possessed himself of so much of the language, religion, and the technique of the civilization of his master as, in his station, he was fitted or permitted to acquire. Eventually, also, Negro slaves transferred their allegiance to the state, of which they were only indirectly members, or at least to their masters' families, with whom they felt themselves in most things one in sentiment and interest.

The assimilation of the Negro field hand, where the contact of the slave with his master and his master's family was less intimate, was naturally less complete.[22]

But, Park was forced to admit, the assimilation was abortive. To account for its shortcomings, he employed the familiar "doctrine of accidents." The postbellum period, he implied, interfered with the black's complete assimilation. Full assimilation, it seemed to him, would have occurred if the Civil War had not broken out, or if the Union had not won. Over and over in his writings Park refers to the good relations that had existed between masters and slaves, to the kindly sentiments and nostalgic feelings which both whites and blacks had for the old days on the plantation. By contrast, he wrote, postbellum race relations were built upon law and formality, ethics and principle, which tended to obviate affection between the races. Formal transactions replaced the earlier ties of real affection and intimacy.

Thus does Park present his case that the postslavery era of American life constituted an obstacle to an assimilation process that had nearly reached its climax. Now a new cycle would begin: Contacts between whites and the now free and mobile blacks would generate in turn conflict, accommodation, and ultimately assimilation. This new cycle would be characterized by new obstacles which, as in the past, might slow down the cycle or halt its progress in certain areas. Among the possible obstacles Park named skin color, black temperament, the rise of racial prejudice among whites, and the failure to establish primary—*i.e.*, intimate—relations across racial lines.

Skin Color

Although Park did not subscribe to the popular hereditary or biological theories of race and behavior, his own observations led him to attach special importance to the effects of skin color on human relations, especially interpersonal understanding. He was fond of referring to William James' essay "A Certain Blindness in Human Beings"[23] to point to man's inability to communicate, empathize with, or intimately know his fellows.[24] "The chief obstacles to the assimilation of the Negro and the Oriental," Park wrote, "are not mental but physical traits" and, in particular, skin color. The faces of blacks and Orientals, he believed, appear masklike to white men.[25] The real person who lives behind the mask might want to make contact, but the mask cannot be taken off and so is forever impenetrable to whites.[26] The impact of a different skin color and facial makeup is to slow down assimilation immeasurably, and in some instances stop it altogether:

> It is not because the Negro and the Japanese are so differently constituted that they do not assimilate. If they were given an opportunity the Japanese are quite as capable as the Italians, the Armenians, or the Slavs of acquiring our culture, and sharing our national ideals. The trouble is not with the Japanese mind but with the Japanese skin. The "Jap" is not the right color.
> The fact that the Japanese bears in his features a distinctive racial hallmark, that he wears, so to speak, a racial uniform, classifies him. He cannot become a mere individual, indistinguishable in the cosmopolitan mass of the population, as is true, for example, of the Irish

and, to a lesser extent, of some of the other immigrant races. The Japanese, like the Negro, is condemned to remain among us an abstraction, a symbol. . . .[27]

Black Temperament

One of Park's persistent themes is racial temperament, which, he wrote, "consists in a few elementary but distinctive characteristics, determined by physical organizations and transmitted biologically."[28] Racial temperament exists, as it were, prior to culture and social organization, and while its expression might be modified by the latter, they cannot alter its basic structure or destroy it. Temperament, Park believed, is made up of innate, unchangeable traits that express themselves concretely through the forms of the culture in which the race finds itself. The manifestations of a racial temperament might change in accordance with general changes in the culture, but the basic element remains intact, "actuated by an inherent and natural impulse, characteristic of all living beings, to persist and maintain itself in a changed environment."[29] Thus, Park concludes, it is of fundamental importance to discover the temperament of a race to know how it will adapt to its environment and just what form its assimilation will take.

Park's thoughts on this subject are, as he said, merely hypothetical.[30] Nevertheless, he was thoroughgoing in his search for the nature of black temperament and suggested that the success of any race-relations policy might very well depend on proper recognition of that temperament. Black temperament was forged in Africa, but because the black had retained so little of his heritage it found a new expression in America. Its nature was most evident in the black church, the "first, and perhaps the only distinctive, institution which the Negro has developed in this country."[31] Park assumed that "the reason the Negro so readily and eagerly took over from the white man his heaven and apocalyptic visions was because these materials met the demands of his peculiar racial temperament and furnished relief to the emotional strains that were provoked in him by the conditions of slavery."[32]

With freedom came changes in external aspects of black temperament, but post-Civil War black churches, schools, and literature were nevertheless only variations on the basic temperament: "The temperament is African, but the tradition is American."[33]

"Out of the mass of cultural materials to which it had access," Park wrote, "the black temperament selected such technical, mechanical, and intellectual devices as met its needs at a particular period of its existence. It has clothed and enriched itself with such new customs, habits, and cultural forms as it was able, or permitted to use. It has put into these relatively external things, moreover, such concrete meanings as its changing experience and its unchanging racial individuality demanded."[34]

What is black temperament? "Everywhere and always," Park wrote, "it has been interested rather in expression than in action; interested in life itself rather than in its reconstruction or reformation." The black is a creature of feelings and presentations, not of action and purposeful social activity. He is, "by natural disposition, neither an intellectual nor an idealist, like the Jew; nor a brooding introspective, like the East African; nor a pioneer and frontiersman, like the Anglo-Saxon. He is primarily an artist, loving life for its own sake. His *métier* is expression rather than action. He is, so to speak, the lady among the races."[35]

One function of black temperament on society has been that of a permanent modifier; as blacks incorporated the culture of white society they also transformed it. From the point of view of the white man's culture, black temperament would limit the fullest possible cultural expression.

Racial temperament also has practical consequences, Park insisted, and policy makers cannot afford to ignore it. "If racial temperament, particularly when it gets itself embodied in institutions and in nationalities, *i.e.*, social groups based upon race, is so real and obdurate a thing that education can only enrich and develop it but not dispose of it, then we must be concerned to take account of it in all our schemes for promotion . . . assimilation . . . and acculturation generally."[36]

Park assumed that racial temperament determines both the individual's vocation and the culture of the race within the society. Speaking specifically on this point, he said that the black in America, "because of his natural attachment to known familiar objects, places, and persons, is pre-adapted to conservatism and to local and personal loyalties. . . . It is certain that the Negro has uniformly shown a disposition to loyalty during slavery to his master and during freedom to the South and to the country as a whole. He has maintained this attitude of loyalty, too, under very discouraging circumstances."[37]

Finally, Park observed, racial temperament is reinforced by segregation and weakened by dispersal. Thus the more absolute the segregation, the purer the temperament, and the longer assimilation will take. He seemed to suggest, then, that if blacks are more fully to incorporate American culture they must leave their isolated communities in the South and their ghettos in the North and come into contact with whites in a wide variety of situations. Barring desegregation and dispersal, the blacks' assimilation would be limited to that capacity and direction dictated by innate temperament.

Racial Prejudice

Park's discussion of prejudice, like his discussion of assimilation and skin color, is vague and inconsistent. At times he spoke of racial prejudice as being a "more or less instinctive and spontaneous disposition to maintain social differences,"[38] or, as he wrote in 1917, "it may be regarded as a spontaneous more or less instinctive defense-reaction, the practical effect of which is to restrict free competition between races."[39] Moreover, prejudice reinforces segregation, which in turn reinforces prejudice:

> When a race bears an external mark by which every individual member of it can infallibly be identified, that race is by that fact set apart and segregated. Japanese, Chinese, and Negroes cannot move among us with the same freedom as the members of other races because they bear marks which identify them as members of their race. This fact isolates them. In the end, the effect of this isolation, both in its effects upon the [groups] themselves, and upon the human environment in which they live, is profound. Isolation is at once a cause and an effect of race prejudice. It is a vicious circle—isolation, prejudice; prejudice, isolation.[40]

Park insisted that racial prejudice does not arise everywhere or among all peoples. Races, of course, first have to be in contact, and prejudice is likely to be precipitated when two races compete for resources or when one race believes its privileges or preserves are being invaded by the other. Racial prejudice is inevitable when a hitherto isolated people migrates to an area where they confront another race which has interests to protect, and the prejudice will persist until a *modus vivendi* ends the competition and establishes a moral order between the quarreling groups. Accommodation, the third stage of Park's race-relations cycle, has thus begun and introduced a racial etiquette: One race has been put into its place.

The degree of racial prejudice in any society, Park pointed out, is relative to the degree of change in the society.[41] Prejudice increases when any low-status group in a previously static social hierarchy demands mobility and recognition and thus threatens to usurp the hard-won privileges of the insecure groups above them. Prejudice, then, "is merely the resistance of the social order to change," Park wrote. "Every effort of the Negro . . . to move, to rise and improve his status, rather than his condition, has invariably met with opposition, aroused prejudice and stimulated racial animosities. Race prejudice, so conceived, is merely an elementary expression of conservatism."[42]

Escalation into racial animosity—direct, active hostility rather than latent prejudice—is a feature of the conflict stage of race relations. "When, however, conflict ceases, when some sort of accommodation of the contending is achieved, animosities subside. In that case the sentiments change. They are no longer hostile, or are only potentially so. On the other hand, the racial prejudices, which are the basis of this hostility, may and often do persist."[43]

Racial prejudice has obviously impeded the black's progress toward assimilation. Its most vicious forms, discrimination and race riots, arose in the contact and conflict stages. In the accommodation stage prejudice assumed a benign form—the racial caste order of slavery. The black's dilemma was that insofar as he would not accept an ignominious caste position, no matter how protective of his life and property it was, and in its place demanded full equality, he upset the accommodated apple cart: He aroused fear and hatred and galvanized into action those very prejudices which had been only a potentiality in the caste society. On the other hand, should the black acquiesce to the caste order and the etiquette it imposed, he would never in his relationships with whites transcend formalities and achieve the interpersonal intimacy necessary for complete assimilation.

Racial prejudice, then, in Park's view is indeed a formidable obstacle, and it was difficult for him to see, given its nature and causes, how blacks could overcome it.

Primary Relations

Of all the obstacles that Park enumerates—and often in his writings they appear as so many *ad hoc* soldiers fighting a losing battle against the ultimately victorious assimilation—the one to which he always returns is the failure of different races to establish primary contact, or interpersonal intimacy.

Interpersonal intimacy was for Park a precondition of the inevitable transition from accommodation to assimilation, and he called it the "great moral solvent." "Interracial friendships," he wrote, "cut across and eventually undermine all the barriers of racial segregation and caste by which races seek to maintain their integrity."[44] Interestingly, he spoke of these interracial intimacies as if they were, in fact, going on and quite common among people of different races engaged in trade and other formal activities. Rarely did Park concern himself with the fact that intimacy between people usually depends on the quality and frequency of their social intercourse. The friendliness he spoke of somehow accompanied the formal arrangements of the accommodation stage yet was distinct from them and overflowed the boundaries of racial etiquette.

In general, Park supposed that the accommodation stage leads to an unobtrusive deepening of interpersonal ties. In their studies of race relations, Park believed, sociologists had been remiss in not reckoning with the effects of personal intercourse and the friendships that inevitably grow up out of them.[45]

For the black, however, Park pointed out that interracial intimacy had already passed its high-water mark. That had occurred during the period of slavery and was most fully evident in the relations between white masters and black house servants. The caste order of slavery had permitted clandestine intimacy and real friendships to arise between slave owners and their human chattels. Indeed, Park argued, this intimacy itself had been about to subvert slavery all by itself. "It was the intimate and personal relations which grew up between the Negro slave and his white master that undermined and weakened the system of slavery from within, long before it was attacked from without. Evidence of this was the steady increase, in spite of public opinion and legislation to the contrary, of the number of free Negroes and emancipated slaves in the South."[46]

After the abolition of slavery the position of the black was that of an erstwhile caste group adrift in a society itself more and more characterized by formality, secondary contacts, and urbanization. But, Park pointed out, this imposed isolation promoted greater intimacy within the black race and a resultant rise of race consciousness. Many blacks now sought a separate self-expression, whether in a federated but independent place within the nation or in a real separation from it. This development was a direct result of the decline of interracial intimacy; it followed and served to reinforce it. Thus assimilation had been deferred, although Park seemed to imply that racial consciousness might be just another substage in the long process of ultimate assimilation.[47]

In the antebellum North, Park argued, black slaves had had an identity in the white mind, but with Emancipation blacks were now an anomaly and provoked an instinctive response, first of apprehension tinged with curiosity, and then of tension. This tension in whites led to "a more vivid awareness and readiness to act—and with that a certain amount of reserve and self-consciousness which is incident to every effort at self-control."[48] This tension is not directly attributable to prejudice or antipathy, although it might produce both. "The strange new creature [encountered by whites] may prove to be attractive, even fascinating. . . . On the other hand, if we seek to get at the very core of this so-called instinctive element in race prejudice, it seems to have its locus just here." A desire to maintain social distance might arise among whites if a black approached them "too suddenly, or if on further acquaintance he seems to behave in outlandish and incalculable ways." In such cases whites are left with "a vague sense of insecurity and malaise which effectually limits intercourse and understanding."[49]

When blacks become in any way importunate there may arise in whites "those antipathies . . . which seem to constitute the most irrational, and at the same time the most invincible, elements in racial prejudice." Insecurity in the presence of the stranger would give rise to apprehension, which would then be organized around racial hallmarks. "Peoples we know intimately we respect and esteem," Park wrote. "In our casual contacts with aliens, however, it is the offensive rather than the pleasing traits that impress us. These impressions accumulate and reinforce natural prejudices."[50]

Only prolonged intimacy can dispel such prejudices, yet, even "after a prolonged and rather intimate acquaintance with an individual of another race, there usually remains a residue of uncertainty and vague apprehension, particularly if the stranger maintains a reserve that we cannot fully penetrate."[51] Consequent attempts to explain racial differences, often by myth and legend, cause the vague fears and anxieties to spiral. "Anything that tends to make a mystery of divergent and alien races . . . tends to intensify antipathies and lend support to racial prejudices."[52]

In this context, Park went on to discuss a major obstacle to intimate black-white relations: the claim by whites that blacks have a unique disagreeable odor.[53] Park did accept the notion "that races and individuals have each a distinctive smell [which] becomes, in certain cases, the sensuous basis for racial antipathies." The man with "a strange, new, pungent odor may arouse disgust, but he may, under other circumstances, evoke a sentiment of awe and respect." Nevertheless, when a strange odor is combined with vague fears and powerful apprehensions, it may lead to disgust and, after that, avoidance.

From smell to touch to fear of mixing the races would seem the natural course, Park concluded. Thus the black is caught in a vicious circle with respect to interracial intimacies. If he seeks them assiduously, he provokes prejudice and antipathy; if he keeps to his own people, he enhances the image of strangeness that already shrouds him and he gives free rein to the myths and legends that purport to describe him. The formal system of racial etiquette persists, and whites remain blinded to his real qualities and individuality.

The Race-Relations Cycle: A Critique

The black seeking his destiny, or a sociologist trying to assist him in assimilating, would find Park's obstacles a tangled thicket. Skin color and temperament seem to be implacable blocks. Moreover, what is done to overcome one obstacle may give rise to another. Thus, while the debilitating aspects of black temperament might be muted by integration, any pushing for intimacy with whites would very likely produce a backlash of prejudice.

Blacks who would look to Park's theory for guidance would discover a host of contradictions and have to confront a variety of excruciating political and moral choices. Advice, in turn, might depend on *post hoc* evaluations of the outcomes of certain trial procedures. For example, if blacks are rebuffed in their attempt to acquire equal social status and intimacy with whites at a given time, Park would explain their failure as a function of one of his "accidents"—*i.e.*, racial prejudice, black temperament, or black skin. Or it might be pointed out that the time was not ripe or else there would have been no rebuff. Such tautological reasoning, which the race-cycle theory encourages, is not likely to promote either sound theory or social change.

Indeed, Park's doctrine of obstacles permits him to draw a radical distinction between events and processes. Nowhere does he cite any racial group that has in fact passed through all the hypothetical stages of his cycle. Instead, the particular situations of a variety of racial groups are merely used to illustrate the several stages individually.

Perhaps the most important criticism to be made of Park's race-relations cycle is that it fails to conform to a canon of empirical science: It cannot be either proved or disproved. As we saw, Park apparently did not accept negative data as a possible refutation of his theory. Perhaps his most revealing statement in this respect was the following, made about Orientals but meant to refer to all races:

> It does not follow that because the tendencies to the assimilation and eventual amalgamation of races exist, they should not be resisted and, if possible, altogether inhibited. On the other hand, it is vain to underestimate the character and force of the tendencies that are drawing the races and peoples about the Pacific into the ever narrowing circle of a common life. Rising tides of color and Oriental exclusion laws are merely incidental evidences of these diminishing distances.[54]

In short, Park attributed any evidence that contradicted his theory to the conservatism of individuals and institutions that could resist inevitable change but never halt it altogether. Everything could be explained away by the doctrine of obstacles.

As Seymour Martin Lipset observed about the problem of demonstrating Park's race-relations cycle, "By their very nature, hypotheses about the inevitability of cycles, whether they be cycles of race relations or the rise and fall of civilization, are not testable at all."[55] And so Park's race cycle over the years has kept sociologists debating. Moreover, it has been waved by liberals seeking to encourage assimilation and wielded by conservatives attempting to stay the progress of blacks.

The Race-Relations Cycle After Park

Ever since Park formulated it, his cycle has been surrounded by unacknowledged confusion, vitriolic debate, and bitter disappointment. Some who have insisted that it is a universally applicable empirical generalization are still puzzled by the way facts seem to elude its net. The works of Louis Wirth[56] and Rose Hum Lee[57] illustrate some of the tangles that arise when Park's cycle is taken as dictum for every ethnic group in America. Both find in their respective empirical studies of Jews and Chinese in the United States that complete assimilation has not in fact occurred.

Wirth attributes the failure of Jews to assimilate in part to anti-Semitism but more significantly to the persistence of distinctively Jewish sentiments and institutions. He manages to regard the latter as "obstacles" to the working out of the Jews' historical destiny in America, and as late as 1945 he had not abandoned his faith that Jews would eventually be assimilated if they would be allowed to fulfill their sociological destiny. Only if hopelessly frustrated, Wirth wrote, would any minority resort to "secessionist tendencies" or "the drive to be incorporated into another state."[58]

Rose Hum Lee is disconcerted to find that after more than a century of settlement in the United States, the

Chinese have not been assimilated into the society. Despite acculturation, Chinese ghettos are still to be found in cities, and although the number of Chinatowns has declined, their population and size have increased. Here Lee contrasts the Chinese with the more rapidly assimilating Japanese and, noting that both groups have suffered prejudice and discrimination, places the blame on the Chinese-American character. Since in recent years hostility against the Chinese has declined, she can only conclude that the failure to assimilate is due in part to Chinatown's elites, who have vested interests in maintaining an exclusive community, but more significantly to a lack of volition among the mass of Chinese-Americans. At the close of her study, Professor Lee exhorts the Chinese to assimilate as rapidly and completely as possible and thus converts Park's prophecy into a plea.

Those sociologists who insist on the empirical validity of Park's race-relations cycle, then, are constrained to account for the failure of various minorities to assimilate as due to obstacles or interferences. However, no study has ever been undertaken to define a set of specific obstacles whose presence would be sufficient to preclude fulfillment of the cycle. Rather, sociologists have tended to introduce whatever event, situation, or attitudinal set has seemed plausible in the case at hand. Park's list of obstacles has been expanded on an *ad hoc* basis, and where none is apparent, mental traits such as lack of will or nerve have been posited. In such a manner some sociologists have thus been able to uphold the theory of the racial cycle in spite of evidence to the contrary.

Park's cycle poses yet another problem for theorists, the question of time. Assimilation will come, but when? Park did not specify how long it would take.

Although they are not adherents of the cyclical theory in its entirety, W. Lloyd Warner and Leo Srole suggest that the time required for assimilation would depend on how close the race in question is in culture and pigment to the dominant race in the society.[59] The greater the difference, the greater will be the subordination of the minority group, the greater the strength and recalcitrance of its subsystem, and the longer the period necessary for assimilation. Warner and Srole define assimilation in terms of language, color, and religion: In the United States, English and Protestantism are dominant in the culture. Color is ranged on a scale from light to dark, with "light Caucasians" at one end and "Negroes and Negroid mixtures" on the other, although exactly why these two are polar is not explained. In any case, according to Warner and Srole, white English-speaking Protestants assimilate rapidly and easily into American society while dark-skinned non-English-speaking groups do so far more slowly, if at all. For blacks, West Indians, Puerto Ricans, and Cubans the rate of assimilation is very slow, and no timetable is given. The narrow scope of this scheme has brought Warner and Srole considerable criticism.[60] For example, the different rates of assimilation of Chinese and Japanese[61] are not accounted for, and, of course, most black Americans already speak English and are, by and large, Protestant.

Other theorists, sufficiently disappointed with the deficiencies in Park's theory, have developed alternative cycles. Emory S. Bogardus developed three distinct cycles to describe the several situations which he found in his researches on the Japanese in California.[62] Jitsuichi Masuoka claimed that for the Japanese in America assimilation takes three generations but that for the third generation, highly acculturated but still not fully accepted, a "genuine race problem arises."[63] W. O. Brown did not accept assimilation as the only outcome of a race-relations cycle but argued that isolation, subordination, and fusion might be alternatives, while assimilation is "perhaps ultimately inevitable but immediately improbable."[64]

Along similar lines of argument but in separate researches, Clarence E. Glick and Stanley Lieberson believe that the final phase of the cycle is problematical and that it might take the form of integration, a nationalist movement, or permanent minority status.[65] Amitai Etzioni goes further than most critics and would abandon Park's race-relations cycle altogether: "While groups are often forced into contact by the process of technological, economic, and social change," Etzioni write:, "and perhaps this is an unavoidable process, the remaining stages [of Park's race-relations cycle] should be seen as alternative situations rather than links in an evolutionary process culminating in assimilation. Groups are either in conflict or accommodation or assimilation."[66]

The failure of facts to corroborate the cycle theory has led some sociologists not only to abandon it but to assert that any theory is impossible in the field of race relations. Brewton Berry stands out here. He is forthright in his criticism of Park and every other sociologist who theorized a race cycle. Berry doubts the existence of any "universal pattern." Rather, he inclines "to the belief that so numerous and so various are the components that enter into race relations that each situation is unique and the making of generalizations is a hazardous procedure."[67] From his own investigations of race relations in Brazil, Hawaii, and between American Indians and whites, Berry concludes that although the course of race relations in these areas is not identical, certain phenomena—conflict, biological mixture, cultural exchange, and domination—are widespread, if not universal.

Finally, some sociologists have chosen to view Park's cycle as a model rather than a theory. Seen thus, the question is how useful is Park's cycle? Is it effective in organizing a vast body of otherwise discrete data, sensitizing sociologists to specific forms of human organization, and generating hypotheses for research? Tamotsu Shibutani and Kian Moon Kwan would answer that there are so many exceptions built into Park's cycle that it can never be verified. However, they find the cycle a "useful way of ordering data on the manner in which immigrants become incorporated into an already-established society." But, they add, there are many exceptions.[68]

E. Franklin Frazier and the Ecology of the Black Family

E. Franklin Frazier (1894-1962) was an early advocate of Park's cycle theory. Over the years Frazier tried to integrate the "scientific" sociology of Park with the tough-minded intellectualism of W. E. B. Du Bois and struggled to fit the facts of black history into Park's theoretical stages. The fruits of his labor are to be found in his ecological study of the black family, his careful study of the emergence of the black as a minority group in American society, and his sociology of race and culture contacts around the world. Although the breadth of his work overflows the bounds of the race cycle and his interests included analyses of the intellectual, cultural, religious, and social life of the black man, the theoretical impetus of his work seems always to have been stimulated by Park's thought on race cycles.

In his study of the black family in Chicago and Harlem, Frazier related the physical patterns of urban growth to the social changes occurring in the race-relations cycle. Park's collaborator on urban studies, Ernest W. Burgess, had described a natural history of city growth and stabilization.[69] According to his view, the city is laid out in five concentric zones. Each zone represents a spatial development of social and cultural forms, and each outward zone is a step upward for the people moving out from the center. Newcomers to the city first live in a factory zone or a nearby transition zone harboring transients, foreigners, unassimilated racial groups, bohemians, and pariahs. As they advance in income, status, and acculturation, they move out into a zone of workingmen's homes, then into a middle-class residential zone, and finally into a commuter zone, the ultimate in urban living.

Turning his attention to the migration of blacks from the South to the urban North, Frazier noticed a similar spatial distribution in the ever-enlarging black ghettos of Chicago and New York.[70] He found in Chicago's ghetto no less than seven zones, in each of which the families exhibited a typical pattern of pushing steadily outward toward the periphery of the ghetto, there to join the economically advancing, culturally assimilating, and racially mixing groups.[71] At the heart of the ghetto dwelt the most demoralized families, unstable economically as well as in every other way, and characterized by a bread-winning mother. Among these the least cultured, most disorganized, and darker black families "with no other resources but their folk culture are ground down by disease, vice, and poverty [while] those possessing intelligence and skill and a fund of family traditions find a chance to rise beyond the caste restrictions of the South."[72] At the edge of the ghetto dwelt the third family type, a stable family having middle-class aspirations, traditional institutional protections, and a fairly heavy admixture of white ancestry.

The movement from zone to zone, Frazier observed, has been a slow, orderly development proceeding in conformity with the race cycle. Moreover, Frazier found evidence of race mixing, the ultimate development of the race cycle: The percentage of mulattoes increased as one moved through the zones and reached its height in areas peripheral to the white parts of the city.

Ever faithful to Park, Frazier explained any failure of this zonal pattern to occur as owing to obstacles or interferences. Traffic patterns, the failure of neighborhoods to deteriorate, the location of certain kinds of

business establishments, or the "long and stubborn resistance" of whites have held back development. Thus Frazier
wrote:

> Although the five zones [of Negro Harlem in New
> York City] indicate the general tendency of the popula-
> tion to expand radially from the center of the com-
> munity, the Negro population has not expanded to the
> same extent in all directions. It has been held in check
> until residential areas have deteriorated and therefore
> have become accessible. . . . In some instances white
> residential areas, even when surrounded by the expand-
> ing Negro population, have put up a long and stubborn
> resistance. This was the case with the area about Mount
> Morris Park. However, when this area lost its purely
> residential character and brown-stone fronts became
> rooming-houses, the eventual entrance of the Negro
> was foreshadowed.[73]

One of Frazier's most telling usages of the doctrine of
obstacles is found in his explanation of why Chicago's
mulattoes, who according to his theory should have been
most numerous in the peripheral zone, showed an unusual-
ly sharp rise in proportionate representation in the third
zone. Under normal conditions this would not happen,
Frazier argues; it was the unique features of this zone that
attracted the high concentration of mulattoes:

> Through the heart of this zone ran Thirty-fifth Street,
> the bright-light area of the Negro community. Here
> were found the "black and tan" cabarets, pleasure
> gardens, gambling places, night clubs, hotels, and
> houses of prostitution. It was the headquarters of the
> famous "policy king"; the rendezvous of the "pretty"
> brown-skinned boys, many of whom were former
> bell-hops, who "worked" white and colored girls in

hotels and on the streets; here the mulatto queen of the underworld ran the biggest poker game on the South Side; here the gambler de luxe ruled until he was killed by a browbeaten waiter. In this world the mulatto girl from the South who, ever since she heard that she was "pretty enough to be an actress," had visions of the stage, realized her dream in one of the cheap theaters. To this same congenial environment the mulatto boy from Oklahoma, who danced in the role of the son of an Indian woman, had found his way. To this area were attracted the Bohemian, the disorganized, and the vicious elements in the Negro world.[74]

Thus, Frazier is saying, mulattoes would have increased proportionally throughout the zones except for the interfering development of a bright-light area in the third zone. In the absence of this interference, the largest proportion of mulattoes would be found in the last zone.

Frazier asserted that his ecological study of the black in Chicago and Harlem not only substantiates Burgess' general theory of urban growth, "that the distribution of human activity resulting from competition assumes an orderly form," but that it also "introduces at the same time an important extension of the theory. It appears that, where a racial or cultural group is stringently segregated and carries on a more or less independent community life, such local communities may develop the same pattern of zones as the larger urban community."[75]

Blacks as a Minority Group: Wirth and Frazier

Louis Wirth, Park's disciple and colleague at Chicago, gave special attention to defining the concept of the minority group and attempted to integrate it with the cycle. Wirth distinguished four types of nationalism[76] found in the modern world: hegemony nationalism, which animates the formation of uniracial and unicultural nation-states; particularistic nationalism, which causes a national minority to seek secession from the state in which it lives; marginal nationalism, which arises among peoples living across the border of the nation to which they adhere culturally and sentimentally; and the nationalism of minorities, which seeks some form of independent existence and cultural expression within the state they inhabit. Particularist nationalism—that is, the drive for secession—is found "in an incipient and utopian form" among Jews and blacks, Wirth observed.

Further, Wirth wrote, the types of orientation which a minority might adopt toward the state are themselves delineated into types: pluralistic, in which a minority seeks toleration for its differences by espousing an ideology holding that variant cultures can live in peaceful coexistence within the nation-state; assimilationist, in which a minority craves complete incorporation into the larger society and discourages any barriers—sexual, social, economic, or political—which might deter this impulse; secessionist, in which a minority repudiates assimilation and, not content with pluralistic toleration, seeks both political and cultural independence from the society it inhabits; and militant, in which a minority seeks as its goal not merely assimilation, toleration, or cultural autonomy but domination over others.[77]

In characteristic fashion, Wirth fashioned several orientations to fit a cycle, which, he observed, "may also be regarded as marking crucial successive stages in the life cycle of minorities generally" and might be employed as a tool "to analyze the empirical problems of minority situations and to evaluate the proposed programs for their solution." Thus:

The initial goal of an emerging minority group, as it becomes aware of its ethnic identity, is to seek toleration for its cultural differences. By virtue of this striving it constitutes a pluralistic minority. If sufficient toleration and autonomy is attained the pluralistic minority advances to the assimilationist stage, characterized by the desire for acceptance by and incorporation into the dominant group. Frustration of this desire for full participation is likely to produce (1) secessionist tendencies, which may take the form either of the complete separation from the dominant group and the establishment of sovereign nationhood, or, (2) the drive to become incorporated into another state with which there exists close cultural or historical identification. Progress in either of these directions may in turn lead to the goal of domination over others and the resort to militant methods of achieving that objective.[78]

In short, the emerging minority would adopt an assimilationist orientation only if no accident frustrated its cultural autonomy and interfered in its progression toward ultimate incorporation within the society. Thus the failure of any minority to assimilate could be explained by reference to the obstacles erected by its own fermenting ethnic consciousness which has found no acceptable outlet. In terms of social policy, minorities might be indulged in bursts of ethnic consciousness insofar as it is expected that this is but a passing phase of their ultimate assimilation.

Frazier's analysis of the black employed Wirth's modification of the race-relations cycle: American blacks are indeed a minority group, and if the obstacles to their ultimate assimilation appear insurmountable, they might develop secessionist orientations and seek political and cultural independence. In developing his argument, Frazier analyzed the nature and extent of the African heritage in

America and the functions of black churches, middle-class status, and the socialization of black youth.

Following Park's lead, Frazier championed the view that the origin and development of the American black subculture lay in slavery and the American environment, not in African cultural forms. In refuting the argument of Melville I. Herskovitz that much of black life is a continuation of African culture, Frazier designated those specific African survivals revealed by Herskovitz and others as remarkable exceptions whose presence only serves to highlight the almost total cultural destruction that slavery had wrought. Although a few language terms, some religious forms, and an occasional social convention of African origin might be found among American blacks, no vestiges of social organization have survived.

Frazier particularly rejected Herskovitz's thesis that the black family structure and certain marital customs and sex practices are African in origin. He argued that the loose and unregulated sex behavior among blacks bears no resemblance to the tradition-directed polygamous cultures of Africa. The matricentric family is a holdover from Africa that received reinforcement under slavery, but slavery had not given support to African ideals of male dominance. Moreover, he argued, the "important picture of the mother in the Negro family in the United States has developed out of the exigencies of life in the new environment. In the absence of institutional controls, the relationship between mother and child has become the essential social bond in the family and the woman's economic position has developed in her those qualities which are associated with a 'matriarchal' organization."[79]

As a first step in his demonstration that blacks are an assimilation-oriented minority, Frazier established that they have very little culture other than that of America. Slavery destroyed the original bondsman's sense of African social organization and his adherence to African kinship systems. Moreover, Frazier stated:

> [Beginning] with emancipation Negroes have from time to time been uprooted from their customary ways of life and have gradually escaped from their isolation . . . they have been affected by the modes of thought and behavior characteristic of civilized or urbanized societies. This has constantly resulted in considerable social disorganization; but at the same time it has led to reorganization of life, at least among certain elements, on a pattern consistent with civilized modes of behavior. During this process of adjusting themselves to American civilization, the majority of the Negroes have sloughed off completely the African heritage.[80]

After slavery, according to Frazier, there was a period of "acute race conflict"[81] which culminated in "accommodation"[82] and ushered in the restoration of white supremacy in the South. The accommodation phase has lasted more than half a century and spawned a proliferation of black communities and a host of black business, labor, and fraternal institutions.[83] In his study of depression-ridden black youth in Louisville, Kentucky, and Washington, D.C., Frazier showed the social and psychological effects of accommodation. Their isolation within segregated settings and their limited opportunities have prevented black young people from transcending the personally destructive ethos which maintains them in their lowly place. But he emphasized their basic accordance with the American system, even to the extent that many accept as true the deprecatory and inferior images which whites employ as justification for discrimination and denial of opportunities.[84]

The black church, Frazier pointed out in a special study, has been an institution of accommodation and a refuge against the onslaught of racial prejudice and urban pressures. But despite resistance, the black church is being inexorably drawn into a world rooted in secularism, impersonality, and demonstrated individual achievement. Assimilation is thus finally coming to pass, for the isolated, authoritarian black church and the other black institutions that have a vested interest in segregation[85] have, until recent changes forced them to conform, constituted a major obstacle to black advancement in democratic processes, interracial experience, higher education, and full incorporation into American society.[86]

Frazier concluded that blacks had emerged as a national minority after World War I. Minority status, he wrote, was the outcome of an unsatisfying condition of accommodation. However, Frazier emphasized that blacks constitute an assimilationist rather than a pluralist, secessionist, or militant minority group. Despite certain sentiments toward pluralism—for example, the widespread support of black masses for Marcus Garvey's Universal Negro Improvement Association[87]—the black man is, as Park had earlier described him, socially and culturally an American:

It is seldom that one finds Negroes who think of themselves as possessing a different culture from whites and that their peculiar culture should be preserved. Perhaps, only in the case of the Negro church where there are vested interests supported by certain cultural traditions, can one find any desire to maintain a separate culture. . . . The Negro has striven as far as possible to efface or tone down the physical differences between himself and the white majority. He does not take seriously the notion of a separate Negro economy. In his individual behavior as well as in his organized forms of social life he attempts to approximate as closely as possible the dominant American pattern. Whenever an opportunity for participation in American culture is afforded, he readily seizes it; that is, so far as his past experiences and preparation permit him to take advantage of such opportunities.[88]

As an assimilation-oriented minority, the black has to overcome obstacles that still block his way into the American mainstream. Frazier does not emphasize skin color and temperament, as Park did, but rather points up the role of racial prejudice and discrimination in staying the black man's progress. These not only deter opportunity, derogate the black's humanity, and deny him the benefits of interracial primary relations, but also contribute to the moral destruction and social disorganization of the black community.[89] Nevertheless, the process of assimilation is proceeding in accordance with a race-relations cycle, although, Frazier wrote in 1957, one more closely approximating Bogardus' seven-stage sequence[90] than Park's original four-stage one. Blacks are in the midst of either the fifth stage, fair-play movements; the sixth stage, acquiescence, presumably something akin to Park's accommodation phase; or the final stage of full assimilation, with variations depending upon the section of the country they inhabit. The general direction of the movement is from integrated secondary relationships in work and politics to intimate interpersonal relationships in friendship and marriage.[91]

Frazier's analysis of black advancement into the middle class is one of the most careful and systematic usages of the original Aristotelian idea of natural change. Aristotle viewed the will of a person or group as subordinate to the immanent natural sources of change which govern its motion. Park employed the same kind of thinking when he spoke nostalgically of the appealing qualities of a caste order at the same time that he predicted its extinction in accordance with the race cycle.[92]

For Frazier the movement of blacks into a black middle class, although it heralds fulfillment of the race cycle's unbreakable promise, is a social and moral tragedy and it occasioned a brooding melancholy in his intellectual mood. Frazier's doleful conclusion—"the black bourgeoisie suffers from 'nothingness' because, when Negroes attain middle-class status, their lives generally lose both content and significance"[93]—is not to be understood as a criticism of black advancement but rather as a commentary on the tragicomic finale dictated by history's irresistible direction. If man is hurt and bewildered when the final curtain falls on the dreaded "nothingness" and ennui of middle-class existence, the fact remains that the scenario has been faithful to the original script. Park once portrayed it as a grand drama of cosmic proportions: "Races and cultures die—it has always been so—but civilization lives on."[94]

Race and Culture Contacts in the Modern World

Frazier, continuing Park's analysis of race relations on the world scene, employed a stage analysis to demonstrate that the outcome of the worldwide cycle would be not as Park envisioned it, a colorless cosmopolitanism, but rather a federation of racial-national cultures.[95] European expansionism had produced three racial frontiers, the Americas, Asia, and Africa. Ensuing imperialism and racial domination generated conflicts on these frontiers, which in turn subsided into accommodative reorganization on the economic, political, and social levels. Ultimately there arose a racial division of labor, multiracial communities within a system of regional autonomy, biracial organizations to mediate or soften the effects of caste and racial prejudice, and variously effective and impatient nationalistic movements.

Mobility will increase the frequency of interracial contacts and perhaps create the conditions for a worldwide community, and interdependence holds out the opportunity for primary relations to arise therefrom. Nevertheless,

Frazier maintains, the three great racial groups—Europeans, Africans, and Asians—will remain spatially isolated and predominant on their respective continents. Although technological uniformity might spread throughout the world, the various racial groups will probably reject the nonmaterial values of Western culture. Cultural homogeneity, an essential feature of assimilation, could perhaps ultimately develop, but for the time being it is held in check by separatist or secessionist nationalism, a powerful obstacle to the working out of universal cosmopolitanism. However, as colonialism based upon color declines, racial differences will assume the aspect of those other differentiations among men that excite interest and curiosity but do not generate ideologies of inferiority or superiority.

"What then will become of the racial frontiers? They will become the areas in which new cultures will ever be born and new peoples will continue the evolution of mankind."[96]

Frazier was not unaware of the theoretical problems posed by the race-relations cycle. He found it more and more difficult to fit the facts of black life into the unilinear history required by the cycle. Confirmation of the cycle depends on events occurring in sequence, and any events running counter to the cycle have to be dismissed as "tendencies" less relevant than those that directly activate or illustrate the cycle's progress. In the end Frazier gave up his search for congruence between history and theory, although his empirical writings suggest a certain implicit, perhaps unconscious, resistance to abandoning sequentialist thinking on the subject.[97] Presenting an outline of his sociology of worldwide racial relations in 1955, Frazier pointed out that:

In referring to stages or phases in the race relations cycle, it is not my intention to suggest that these stages represent a chronological order in the development of race relations. Since these different stages in the race relations cycle may exist simultaneously, they represent logical steps in a systematic sociological analysis of the subject. My analysis will take account of the dynamic factors—demographic, economic, political, and social—which would rule out any notion of a unilinear evolutionary process.[98]

Frazier appears to have been well on the way to resolving one of the most onerous theoretical problems of the race-relations cycle—its invulnerability to empirical investigation. Sociologists employing the cycle have introduced the doctrine of obstacles to account for events antithetical to the cycle. However, if obstacles are introduced indiscriminately and on an *ad hoc* basis, the cycle becomes untestable as a theory, since no evidence whatever can be used to refute it.

One way out of this dilemma would be to construct a finite and definite set of ideal-typical interferences whose presence would constitute an adequate explanation of the failure of the predicted state of affairs to materialize. Thus, assimilation will occur unless x occurs, where x is an unambiguous and specific element contained in the theory itself.

Frazier's final concept of the cycle as a set of logical rather than chronological steps and his exploration of what he calls the dynamic factors—specific demographic, economic, political, and social elements present in any situation—bid fair to encourage the formulation of that limited and definite set of interferences which would convert Park's untestable cycle into a hypothesis capable of empirical validation. Frazier's untimely death may have cut off a theoretical breakthrough of major significance for the sociology of race relations.

Conclusion

Robert E. Park synthesized the thought of the Social Darwinists who preceded him and the social-problems theorists who continued to point to obstacles to progress. In his theory, race relations proceed according to the directives of an evolutionary unilinear cycle beginning in racial contact and continuing through conflict and accommodation until ultimately race relations disappear as such in the culminating stage, assimilation.

In concluding our remarks on this subject we must distinguish between the theory's effect on blacks, and its effect on the sociology of the black man. Park's cycle was capable of holding out promise to an oppressed people at the same time that it might be used to retard progress in social amelioration. Hope of a raceless universe devoid of prejudice and racial animosity could give some comfort to those who suffer in the mundane world of fruitless toil and hostility. Moreover, it might inspire some to action in behalf of aiding, perhaps even hastening, the forces of history. On the other hand, Park's cycle could be employed to justify the status quo and oppose any moves to change it. History here is perceived as moving according to its own unchangeable and secret dynamic: Whatever state of affairs exists does so because it cannot be otherwise. Attempts to change the present situation can only result in failure because those changes that are meant to come about will do so when and because they are meant to. Men cannot change or hasten the fate intended for man. For some, Park's cycle has held out the promise of mastering society; for others, it has provided intellectual justification for inaction while they wait history's end to reveal itself.

Park inspired a generation of sociologists to examine the possibility that the black man was about to be ushered into the assimilation stage of the race-relations cycle. For the most part these sociologists found little evidence of the event. In their disappointment some held out hope by devoting their attention to obstacles that had thus far held back assimilation; others reformulated the cycle or attempted to perceive it as a model rather than a theory; still others abandoned all faith in cyclical theories.

More than any other sociologist, Frazier attempted to fit the facts of black history to the race-relations cycle and to show the obstacles to black assimilation. Eventually his researches brought him close to penetrating the theory's Achilles' heel—its resistance to proof. Frazier was perhaps on the brink of formulating a set of conditions under which the cycle might be empirically tested rather than merely "validated" by appeal to an infinite set of interferences.

Park's cycle has detoured sociologists around the systematic study of black history. Since the events of that history are supposed to conform to cyclical dictates, there has been considerable incentive among sociologists to select out those events that fit the cycle and to designate all others as accidental and irrelevant. Rather than developing hypotheses against which the evidence might be presented, sociologists tended to reverse the process and present evidence selectively in accordance with the already accepted theory of the race cycle. To take one instance, Park supposed that accommodation set the stage for those intimate relationships that would erode distinctions of caste and race. But he never tested this proposition, and thus he cut off sociological investigation at precisely that point where it should have begun—at the institutions wherein intimate contact presumably takes place, in schools, jobs, and other situations of secondary contact.

The Aristotelian ideas of change are the familiar furniture of the sociological mind. They have given impetus to theories of development and cycles that encourage disdain of the historical record and insistence on the logic of *a priori* conception. So long as this practice continues, the historical record will remain largely unexamined and the reality of black life will be inadvertently suppressed in the name of a conjectural history's "natural" dictates.

III

SOUTHERN GOTHIC: CASTE AND RACE IN SOUTHERN SOCIETY

ALTHOUGH Robert E. Park was concerned with the outcome of the race-relations cycle and often spoke in apocalyptic terms of the final stage of worldwide assimilation, he was just as much concerned with the intermediate stages of conflict and accommodation. Late in his life he returned to the idea of conflict and spoke of the inevitable necessity for blacks to struggle for full equality. Such a struggle, he argued, would promote not only race interests but the survival of democracy itself:

Democracy is not something that some people in the country can have and others not have, not something to be shared and divided like a pie—some getting a small piece and some getting a large piece. Democracy is an integral thing. If any part of the country has it they all have it, if any part of the country doesn't have it, the rest of the country doesn't have it. The Negro in fighting, therefore, for democracy is simply fighting the battle for our democracy.[1]

Many whites want to restrict democracy to themselves and will work to subvert the blacks' struggle; even liberals want to slow down the process of democratization for blacks because they fear disorders. "If conflicts arise as a result of the efforts [of blacks] to get their place it will be because the white people started them," Park writes.

"These conflicts will probably occur and are more or less inevitable but conditions will be better after they are over."[2]

Accommodation in America has consisted of that unequal division in democracy which, Park says, results in no democracy at all. Nevertheless, accommodation, insofar as it is socially sanctioned—a tacit social contract between races that are antagonistic toward each other—serves to maintain order.

That at certain moments in history order and democracy need not coincide seems to have been one of Park's more prescient perceptions. "Every society," he writes, "represents an organization of elements more or less antagonistic to each other but united for the moment, at least, by an arrangement which defines the reciprocal relations and respective spheres of action of each."[3]

Accommodation not only reduces tension and affords a *modus vivendi* for the contending parties; it also secures a recognizable identity for the individual and temporary stability for the race. However, Park points out, all accommodations are inherently unstable, dependent as they are on the status quo. "With a change in the situation, the adjustment that had hitherto successfully held in control the antagonistic forces fails. There is confusion and unrest which may issue in open conflict."[4] The new conflict would result in yet another form of accommodation, and this conflict-accommodation-conflict sequence would continue until such time as the disaffected groups become homogeneous. "It is only with assimilation that the antagonism, latent in the organization of individuals or groups, is likely to be wholly dissolved."[5]

Park's observations about the nature and role of accommodation gave impetus to a host of studies on the social order in the South. According to the views presented in these studies, social organization in the post-Reconstruction South constituted an accommodation of latent race conflicts of remarkable proportions. Seething animosities between blacks and whites were held in check by a system of institutional segregation, racial etiquette, and custom which was enforced ultimately by fear and periodically by terror. As long as this state of affairs remained untouched by conscious interference or by evolution of the society itself, the hatred between the races did not erupt into open warfare.

Some of the studies of the Southern social order were carried out by psychoanalytically oriented anthropologists, sociologists, and psychologists. A psychoanalytic movement among American intellectuals had begun in the 1920's, and in the next decade its effects were felt in the social sciences. American social institutions came under serious psychoanalytic scrutiny, which was intensified by the arrival in America of Freudian scholars fleeing from Nazism.[6] In general these studies reflected the attempt to link social structure and frustration. The basic idea had been presented in Freud's *Civilization and Its Discontents*: Society itself generates frustration since, by its very nature and operation, it suppresses impulses and restricts individual freedom.

In the South anthropologists found a special instance of this sociopsychoanalytic theorem: The caste system that had grown up to accommodate relations between the politically powerful whites and the subordinated but restive blacks engendered deep-seated frustrations. Ordinarily, such frustrations would lead to aggressive impulses. In the case of blacks, however, aggressive acts had to be inhibited and thus a new round of frustration and aggression resulted. Ethnographers took a different tack: They sought to discover the positive functions of the caste system—the "gains" which each group obtained from accommodation—and thus to elucidate the elements which sustained a system of racial subordination.

John Dollard's Caste and Class in a Southern Town

John Dollard received his PhD from the University of Chicago in 1931. Undoubtedly his intellectual development was influenced by the sociological school there, but his special interests were reinforced and given direction by his psychoanalytic studies at Yale with Clark Hull. Hull had sought to achieve a synthesis of conditioning theory and psychoanalysis, and Dollard, who had himself been analyzed by Hans Sachs in Berlin, developed a keen interest in applying psychoanalytic concepts to the study of groups and communities. In 1937 he published his most significant intellectual labor, the psychoanalytic ethnography of "Southerntown," a community of some 2,500 inhabitants.[7] His principal object was to "reveal the main structure of white-Negro adjustment in Southerntown from the standpoint of emotional factors."[8]

Adjustment in Southerntown, Dollard begins, has been made in the form of caste accommodation. However, this mode of adjustment is irreconcilable with professed "American" values, and thus there "is a conflict between the dominant American mores, which are expressed formally in the Declaration of Independence, and the regional mores of the South which have had to deal with the Negroes." This conflict, Dollard continues, "has done more than any other to wrack the American constitutional system, and it is still one of the major sources of unbalance in our social life. The present-day continuation of this dilemma is plainly visible in Southerntown and is an aspect of the personal lives of all its people."[9]

The caste order of Southerntown finds its most fundamental expression in the rigidly enforced customs of racial endogamy. Blacks cannot marry whites, and white women cannot take black men as paramours or sex partners of any kind, although white men might discreetly dally with black women. Sex mores are a kind of signpost to all racial relationships; hence trespass on them constitutes a serious breach and evokes severe sanctions.

In America, Dollard observes, caste is based on biological rather than cultural characteristics: skin color, hair texture, and other physiognomic features constitute caste marks. Moreover, a caste order exists not only within the society as a whole but also within the black caste itself. "White" characteristics are often admired by blacks. Lighter-colored blacks are given status within the race, and dark-skinned blacks indicate some self-hatred or embarrassment about their hue. It is not uncommon for black parents to urge their children to "marry light" or to attribute failures in social life, business, or marriage to the effects of dark or Negroid features.

The caste order between the races is maintained by rigid segregation in education and religion and by excluding blacks from participation in political and civic activities. Southerntown boasts a fine black high school facility, a rarity in the area, but it lacks a fourth year and has a defective curriculum. Black colleges must then assume the burden of making up for the deficiencies in their students' education.

> The seeming purpose of the educational system as modified by caste and class in the South is to train whites for their class and caste positions of mastery and responsibility; hence, on the whole, they are better trained. Since Negroes in turn are trained for their expected lower-caste positions in the system, they receive the simpler, more manual and practical forms of training. . . . This difference in training is not always realized in fact and doubtless a little algebra and history filter in along with the manual training and applied agriculture. Caste training is, nevertheless, the theory if not the fact of educational practice in Southerntown.[10]

Nevertheless, Dollard emphasizes, there have been substantial advances in the number of blacks enrolled in school, in the educational qualifications of teachers, and in educational uplift.

Dollard suggests that black education bids fair to undermine the caste system that presently maintains the social order. As blacks acquire skills and abilities and realize that they can perform the same tasks as whites, they perceive the senselessness and hostility of the caste system. Education, then, portends at least a latent subversion of racial accommodation in the South.

According to Dollard, the growth of the separate black church provides "the best example of bi-racialism, that is, of a social order divided in all its functions along caste lines."[11] As a counterpart to a powerful white institution, the black church offers a vicarious mode of achievement and mobility, thus performing an invaluable psychological function for a people bowed down by caste restrictions, and it serves as a training ground for leadership on a truly democratic and equalitarian basis. Because black churches serve an educational as well as a spiritual function, they open the door to the black colleges in the South, which are largely denominational. In its role as educator, Dollard suggests, the black church, created to conform with the caste order, may actually serve to undermine it.

The hints of weakness in the caste system which characterize Dollard's discussion of education and religion are not found in his analysis of Southerntown's politics. In that arena the caste order seems to be impermeable both to subversion and direct attack: Southerntown employs the poll tax, the educational qualifications test, and the "white primary" to exclude blacks from the voting booth.

Among Southerntown's whites, consciousness of their own history during Reconstruction colors all discussions of voting behavior. The integrated legislature and the state's black representatives in Congress in that period are regarded as a tragedy of major proportions, a degradation imposed by their Yankee conquerors. Dollard appears to share some of their concerns, and it is perhaps remarkable to find him referring to the "fascistic rule of the northern armies" which made it possible "to keep the bottom rail on top."[12]

Although whites usually justify exclusion of the black man from the polls on the grounds of his supposed ignorance and tractability or by reference to possible black domination should blacks be allowed to exercise their numerical majority, Dollard points out the real reason: "From our standpoint there is an easy answer as to why Negroes are not allowed to vote: it would upset the present-day caste relationships and the gains dependent on them, it would damage white prestige, and it would open the door to social (sexual) equality."[13] The politics of Southern caste, then, exist for the purpose of providing continuous support to a system which has direct material and symbolic value to white citizens.

Dollard's analysis of what he calls the gains achieved by the caste order constitutes one of the most significant sociopsychological explanations for the continued existence of that system. First, he rejects the static thesis presented earlier by W. I. Thomas and Florian Znaniecki[14] to account for social stability in any way of life. According to this theory, a pattern of behavior is established at a given historical moment and continues to operate until some event or process disorganizes it.

Dollard argues that a system must have some payoffs for its members and that in order to survive an imbalance of advantages and disadvantages, it must be weighted on the side of the former. In the case of the Southern racial castes, whites receive economic, sexual, and prestige gains. Blacks, who are subjected to white domination and general deprivation, nevertheless receive certain advantages that derive from subordinate status.

Dollard sees the economic gains of the caste order as twofold. Whites, defined as the superior caste group, do little of the heavy, back-breaking labor associated with construction or maintenance and almost never engage in the socially degrading and physically exhausting work of cotton picking. Menial labor, cotton picking, and domestic work are done by blacks, and this in turn defines and justifies their social location in the lower caste.

The extent of the second economic gain is relative to the wealth of a region. Southerntown is a poor area, and the culture of poverty is apparent in some degree among all its citizens. Nevertheless, the whites have devised multifarious ways by which to keep blacks financially dependent on them. The use of company stores, payment in kind, the "furnish system" for sharecroppers, and abuse of domestic servants all contribute to the asymmetrical distribution of wealth and status.

Blacks do object to the system, and sometimes forcibly. When this occurs, however, countervailing power of greater magnitude is employed. An informal surveillance is kept over the black community, and labor organizers, Northern reformers, and black nationalists are chased out of the area. A widespread belief that blacks are lazy, improvident, and shiftless serves to rationalize the dependency relations created by the system, as well as to justify the whites in their benevolent "protection" of "their" blacks from the "abuses" which would inevitably occur if Yankee agitators were to obtain influence over them. (Dollard suggests that the stereotype of the Southerntown black may be a valid description, because the whites, whose economic future is contingent on black dependency, discourage habits of thrift, responsibility, and hard work and indulge blacks in their loose and unregulated social life within the black community. In the North, he asserts, where status advancement is a real incentive, and where the caste barrier is both less explicit and less rigid, blacks do not manifest stereotypical behavior.) The economic gains of the caste system in the South, then, encourage a way of life that reinforces the rationale of the system itself.

The sexual gain provides white men, by virtue of their superior caste position, with two classes of women—white women, from whom they draw their sweethearts and wives, and black women, of whom they take sexual advantage. Of course, Dollard points out, by the same caste code of sexual conduct, black women have access to white men, while white women and black men are required to find partners from among their own racial group.

Thus the caste barrier enables white men to conserve their own sexual property—*i.e.,* white women—and at the same time enjoy sexual access to black women, whereas black men are unable to protect their wives, daughters, and sisters from white men's advances and have little opportunity for sex relations with white women. "In sum, it seems to be true that the white-caste member experiences a sense of gratification in this mark of his caste mastery, his preferential access to two groups of women and immunity to the resentment of the disadvantaged Negro men."[15]

Dollard's analysis of the reciprocal sex gains of whites and blacks is a creative contribution to psychoanalytic sociology. He suggests that the idealization of white womanhood in the South, combined with the degraded image of black women, represents a dual image of women that allows whites to maintain their ideals and yet indulge their sexual impulses. White women are preserved and protected in accordance with a chaste stereotype, while black women, regarded almost as a separate species, are used to relieve sexual desires.

But black women too may find a gain in this situation, because they are freer to express otherwise inhibited sexual impulses and are protected from reproach because they dare not refuse a white man's bidding. Moreover, by having sexual relations with white men, black women may achieve an otherwise forbidden sense of equality with whites or a sense of degrading these same white men who hold them in disrepute.

It is black men who suffer a sense of real deprivation and demoralization. They cannot protect their own women, and this indignity compromises their manhood. And they are constrained from revenge against white men because of their sure knowledge of the consequences should they be accused, however falsely, of rape. In Southerntown white men achieve another sense of their own mastery by their access to two classes of women, black women may gain a clandestine sexuality and secret revenge, and black men are the losers.

Southerntown's caste order, Dollard writes, might be defined as a "systematic program for enhancing the self-abnegating reactions of Negroes."[16] It also provides a prestige gain for whites. Dollard's analysis shows a psychological reciprocity in the deferential behavior of blacks toward whites. Whites are confirmed in the image of their own superiority, and blacks obtain that peculiar mastery enjoyed by the servant over his master. However, not all blacks adopt ignominious postures. "Uppity" blacks, as the whites define those who refuse to show proper deference, are dealt with most severely: They might be assaulted, fired from their jobs, expelled from the community, or killed. The demand for deference from others may be a universal trait, but the occasions for it vary according to culture. "In the North a man may have a prestige position because he has money, or is learned, or is old," Dollard writes. "The novelty in the South is that one has prestige solely because one is white."[17]

Whites realize an enhancement of the self when blacks, rigidly following the racial etiquette of the South, indicate their own lowliness and the white man's superiority.

Dollard compares this inflated self-image with the illusion of greatness sometimes experienced in the early stages of drunkenness: "It gives not only the sense of sweet submissiveness of others, but also a gratifying sense of mastery. For anxious persons it may tend also to create a feeling of security in being, or appearing to be, so well loved."[18]

Moreover, the dreaded fear of black antipathy toward whites is allayed by a subservient demeanor. By being deferential the black shows that he is not hostile, Dollard writes. "Whites are not satisfied if Negroes are cool, reserved, and self-possessed though polite; they must be more than polite; they must be actively obliging and submissive. It would seem that there is much fear behind the demand of white people for submissiveness on the part of Negroes."[19]

Why do blacks give the deference that is so gratifying to whites? Dollard sees two possible motives. The first is based on the familiar idea that repressed hostility is often concealed by servile behavior: The repressed antagonism may be an essential response to the need for self-abnegation. The second motive is a perverse desire to identify with a socially powerful white person, which, Dollard writes, is "accompanied by idealization, pride in the white man, permissiveness, and a wish to serve him. Eventually this second motive gives rise to a wish to be like the white man."[20] This idealization of the white man forces the black into a deflection from that natural primary narcissism which would idealize the distinctive features of his own race. Blacks are impelled by caste requirements to suffer a "narcissistic wound" and to learn to prefer white color and features to their own.[21] The depth of this wound is revealed in the neuroses and psychoses from which some blacks suffer and to which the color caste makes all blacks prone.

Dollard does not explain the origins of the caste system, except for a brief allusion to its beginnings in slavery. What he does argue is that its operation in the contemporary South is habitual and, "by and large, people conform to it, both white and Negro, because they must. The white person in Southerntown has no more option about calling a Negro 'Mr.' than the Negro has to demand the title."

Violation of the caste system can bring severe reprisals, even death. However, intimidation is usually sufficient to guarantee compliance. Blacks have learned to accommodate themselves to the system and thereby gain some small measure of security and occasional profit. Dollard emphasizes three modes of accommodation: Blacks might suppress their aggressive impulses toward whites and substitute in their stead passive attitudes of subservience and compliance; blacks might give up the competition to obtain the rights, privileges, and prerogatives of white people and accept instead those forms of gratification that arise out of their own lower caste position; or blacks might redouble their efforts to rise in the class system of their own caste, hoping to secure class equality with whites within an unchanged biracial caste system.

The socialization of blacks into Southerntown's caste-oriented culture requires them to renounce belief in equality of opportunity, devalue their own physical characteristics, remember their fixed place in the caste order, and squelch any sense of resentment about these renunciations. They must reorganize their character, Dollard writes, "so that protest does not appear, but acceptance does."[22] The final product of a "successful" socialization is a façade of unquestioning acceptance of the white man's conception of the social order. However, Southerntown's mores are not the only source from which blacks derive a sense of identity; they are also aware of the equalitarian ideals that make up the national culture. As a result they are caught up in the dilemmas and contradictions of a dual identity system, and they must forge a personal identity and a social character to suit the several situations in which they find themselves.

Out of this peculiar condition blacks have created a sort of double character—one for presentation before whites, the other, a more "genuine" one, which emerges within the black community. In the first characterization the black typically employs a high-toned, pleading voice full of uncertainty and a variety of deference forms and terms of address which accord high status to whites and degrade blacks. Among blacks the forms are actively cultivated; the entire orientation, "the white-folks manner," is regarded as an essential tactic in the tacit struggle between the races. Concealment of his actual thoughts is the crucial component of the black's façade, but, while it protects him from revealing his true feelings of hostility, it also encourages the view that he is treacherous and sly. The accommodative form reaches its quintessential development in white patronage of a black. By ingratiating himself to a white man, a black acquires an "angel" who provides him with favors and privileges for which he is otherwise ineligible. But, Dollard observes, patronage has its price. "The 'angel' will protect only a properly deferential Negro."[23]

Among the blacks of Southerntown, magic is a source of private power and an important ingredient in buoying up their spirits. The purpose of magic—employing charms, potions, lucky and unlucky days, etc.—is to gratify a wish for love, power, revenge, or other fulfillment that is unattainable in actuality. Magic does not upset the existing caste order; rather, it takes the place of just those things that would—political agitation, black racial solidarity, or other concerted action that would change status relationships. As a set of symbolic and expressive activities, magic serves psychological functions of considerable importance: It provides an outlet for fantasy and gives comfort to a people seemingly helpless in the face of white domination.

In Southerntown there is no attempt to iron out differences through biracial meetings, since whites jealously guard their monopoly over decision making against any encroachments by blacks. Whatever concessions are made to blacks are at the behest of whites. However, the caste system is undermined by the contradictory customs which Southerntown's blacks discover when they travel to the North. To the extent that travel to the North continues, or that news about its less rigid caste order is communicated, Southerntown's blacks are made aware of a different way of life which might be their own. Travel and news provide "a type of experience which liberates aggression and tends to translate a passive accommodation to the status quo into an active demand for new opportunity," Dollard writes. "Accommodation to the caste system tends to be broken up as new ideals of personal dignity and freedom are concretely understood by Negro individuals."[24]

The caste order frustrates blacks in their desire for dignity, status, power, and self-sufficiency. Normally, frustrations are followed by aggressive acts against the persons, objects, or institutions which produce them. But in the case of the black, aggression must be inhibited, since even a sign of hostile feelings subjects him to the wrath of the white man. Blacks learn to cloak their hostile feelings, and this in turn leads to a deflection of aggression onto other blacks.

Aggression within the black community most commonly takes the form of beatings, knifings, and homicides inflicted by men upon their rivals for a woman's affections, upon the woman herself, and on children. Black women are frequently the victims of assaults by jealous members of their own sex. In analyzing this aggression Dollard places great emphasis on its source in deflected hostility toward whites. Black men, unable to protect their own women, and also unable to avenge themselves on the white predators, direct their rage at their black rivals and at black women, who, subjected to sexual intercourse with white men, symbolize the black man's impotence.

The fights over gambling, the aggressive banter, and the sometimes deadly verbal contests are features of black lower-class behavior arising in part from the unstable marriages common to this class and the almost Homeric idealization with which these blacks view physical strength and skills in self-defense. However, Dollard notes, as blacks ascend to the middle class, family life is strengthened, greater value is placed on inhibition of hostile impulses, and care is taken to dissociate themselves from the aggressive traits which are commonly imputed to blacks in the lower class.

Not only does the caste order create the conditions for black hostility and then blunt the expression of that hostility, but it also creates a double standard of justice and law enforcement. Crimes committed by blacks against whites are punished with greater severity than the same crimes involving only whites. But criminal activity within the black community is overlooked; to whites it is simply further proof of the blacks' "savagery." As a result, blacks come to prize those skills of pugnacity and violence that are required for the brutish life of segregated existence. Moreover, Dollard points out, whites are aware that one function of the aggression among blacks is to reduce chances of black solidarity, which, should it arise, might overthrow the entire racial caste system of the South.

Since blacks are well aware of the sanctions against direct aggression toward whites, they frequently resort to circuitous forms to express their hostility. And, because black indirectness arouses white suspicions, accidents and ambiguous events are interpreted as signs of hostility, of "uppity" behavior, or of carefully planned aggression. Moreover, whites sometimes goad blacks beyond the point of endurance and then severely punish them for the ensuing infraction. In retaliation blacks employ surreptitious methods of avenging themselves on whites. One is to ambush a white man after dark. Another is to rape white women, a crime whose impulse, says Dollard, is rooted in the black's unconscious as the best possible revenge against the overbearing domination of the white caste.

Beyond these not very subtle modes of revenge and aggression are all those artful forms of speech, gossip, jokes, stories, and fantasies by which blacks can express their anger and achieve a modicum of return for their lowly and miserable existence. As Dollard shows, the caste order creates a condition of frustration, impels a system of deflected aggression, but cannot itself dictate precisely all the forms, delicate and devious, that this repressed aggression will take.

Perhaps Dollard's most important contribution is his analysis of black gains in the caste system. True to his original thesis, Dollard attempts to show that the Southern system of white racial domination provides certain advantages to blacks that might not accrue in a more equalitarian system. He argues that lower caste position provides opportunities for liberty and license denied to upper castes. Precisely as a result of their superior station in life, whites must deny themselves permanent dependency relationships, forgo the more extravagant pleasures of the flesh, and inhibit impulsive expressions of aggression. But blacks may indulge their impulses inside the freewheeling black community; in fact, they are expected to do so.

As Dollard sees it, the secret advantage of being a black in the Southern caste order is that it affords one the opportunity to practice life much nearer to its primordial psychobiological baseline: Blacks come closer to realizing the advantages of sexual freedom, emotional liberty, and unrestrained impulsiveness than do other higher-status groups. The white man may envy the black's unbridled existence, may even see it as the truly free life. At the same time, he is bitter that this "parasitic" race benefits from the technology of white society and is "able to indulge extraordinary impulse freedom at the expense of the nervous energy and moral renunciation of the white upper classes."[25]

To the extent, then, that the social tendency in the United States is toward elevation of everyone, including blacks, into the middle class, it will force lower-class blacks to give up the sociopsychological gains obtained from their pariah position.

Dollard concludes his study with an analysis of the social and psychological sources of racial prejudice. His psychoanalytic training places a perspective on his sociological interpretation which makes up in penetration what it loses in one-sidedness.

Whites perceive the black as a child, Dollard writes, and this perception produces a doubly significant result. It permits whites to arrogate to themselves the role of parents and to derogate blacks by indulging them in precisely that kind of behavior associated with children—idleness, irresponsibility, promiscuousness. Whites perceive themselves as having duties toward the childlike blacks, while blacks, either as a guileful tactic or as an automatic response of accommodative socialization, perform their requisite roles as "children."

The caste order identifies the whites as mature and, as ratification of this, delegates power, privilege, and responsibility to them; it imputes to blacks a childlike ambivalence to their elders, a mischievous or aggressive orientation, and an unwarranted desire to be treated like grownups. A caste system, Dollard writes, "is a categorical barrier on growing up. . . . There is one very important difference between the Negro and the child. The inferior status of the white child is temporary and the hope of personal maturity is present, sure and strong; with the Negro the status of the child is confirmed and chronic, and there is no hope of escaping it."[26]

In any society, Dollard continues, restrictions placed on children and inhibitions imposed on adults create deep frustration, which in turn generates hostilities that if expressed directly on their true sources would break up the social organization itself. Racial prejudice thus plays a role in maintaining the social order by providing a target on which to deflect these hostilities without violating the generally held taboo on aggression against one's group. Because they may be disliked without guilt, because they are defenseless, blacks are an eligible target for hatred and scorn, victims of the white man's free-floating aggressions.

The alternatives to racial prejudice, Dollard suggests, involve either an inversion of aggression toward oneself, which would most likely be productive of neuroses, or the substitution of a moral equivalent of blacks—*i.e.,* some other target against whom aggressions might be flung. Since the likelihood of either of these solutions to the race problem is slight, it would appear that the accommodative caste order will continue to operate for some time.

In his introduction to the third edition (1957) of *Caste and Class in a Southern Town*, Dollard writes that the single most significant lag in race relations has been the failure of blacks to move into the middle class of their own caste order:

> The *evolutionary* change which can now occur, and be furthered by human resolution, is to move larger and larger numbers of Negroes into the middle class of their caste. Economic factors seem at the present time to favor this change. Continued pressure to equalize educational opportunities as between Negroes and whites can also aid. Similarly, the effort to make our Government, at least, evenhanded and neutral in its treatment of Negro citizens should be pressed vigorously by all those who realize that change is inevitable but wish to bring it about in an orderly manner.[27]

Despite his belief that the threat of Communism is forcing an ever greater urgency on America to solve the race problem and that "Americans instinctively hate the caste system and will not too long abide it,"[28] Dollard concludes that revolutionary ways of solving the problem are not feasible. Since a "revolutionary" solution would "solve the Negro problem, like the 'white' problem, by a scorching tyranny,"[29] blacks should be urged to await their eventual liberation with patience:

> In the American evolutionary scheme, every ethnic group has had to stand in line, to endure the cruel paring of beloved cultural habits, to work and wait for assimilation. In one sense, therefore, the Negro has met the same fate as every other ethnic group which has been introduced to the society. . . . The caste system [however] would relegate the Negro *forever* to an inferior position in the society [and] must be abandoned. The Negro may have to wait, but he must know that he has a future in American society and that he *can* attain the same goal of dignified participation which is held out to other Americans.[30]

Conclusion

Under the influence of Park and his associates a number of studies on the black in the South emerged, many of which have enduring value despite the sometimes shaky theoretical assumptions that inspired them. Specifically, these studies sought to uncover the enduring qualities of the Southern caste order and to locate the sources and consequences of institutionalized racism in that region. That institutionalized caste racism has a territorial enclave in the South was an undisputed presupposition of these researches. That the caste order provides advantages not only to the dominant white group but also, in subtle and peculiar ways, to the subordinated blacks was one of the most important findings. Moreover, psychoanalytic theory provided a new dimension for understanding social structures.

Unfortunately, the same perspectives that opened new doors to understanding the social order also closed off opportunities for a comprehensive knowledge of the origins of racism.

Dollard's *Caste and Class in a Southern Town* is perhaps the most important study of the processes, functions, and maintenance of accommodation in the South.

Charles S. Johnson's *Shadow of the Plantation*,[31] which Dollard drew on extensively in his own work, describes patterns of family, educational, economic, and folk life among plantation blacks, exposes the enforced system of racial etiquette that governed their lives, and places great emphasis on technological innovations and cultural lag in explaining the changes in black life. Ultimately it suggests a planned agricultural economy as the source for black liberation from isolation and poverty.

Davis, Gardner, and Gardner's *Deep South: A Social Anthropological Study of Caste and Class*[32] stresses the two class systems that exist within the biracial caste order. More than Dollard they emphasize the role of power and the veiled threat of force that ensure caste-order maintenance.

Hortense Powdermaker's *After Freedom: A Cultural Study in the Deep South*[33] provides a useful check on Dollard's work, since it was carried out in the same town as his study and at the same time but by an anthropologist. Powdermaker had better entree into the black community than Dollard and wrote her study with less paternalism and more empathy than he. She describes "Cottonville's" blacks as going through the acculturative process of becoming sociologically white while remaining physically black and details the responses, which differed by generational group, to this paradoxical phenomenon.

Johnson and Davis and Dollard, in separate publications, documented the socialization processes of black youth, emphasizing the ever-present domination of the white caste as a deterrent to development of black self-esteem and the differentiating effect of class status within the caste for self-identity and social orientation.

In all of these studies, and some that came after—such as Hylan Lewis' excellent *Blackways of Kent*[34]—we find the same emphasis on the South as a peculiar subculture of American life, on the contradiction between the general American mores and those of this caste-ridden region, and on the dilemmas—personal and social—that arise out of living with or trying to change the old social order.

Common to the studies of these social scientists is the belief that the South is characterized by a peculiar social order not found outside of it: The principal characteristic of the Southern system is its caste barrier between the races, which is rooted in desires for racial endogamy and governed by a system of institutional apartheid and social degradation of the black man. They further assume that in the North no caste barriers exist to any great extent and that, instead, racial prejudice, whose psychodynamics are a feature of personality development and socialization errors, constitutes the greatest obstacle to black advancement. This distinction between racial prejudice and caste prejudice, they conclude, distinguishes the American regions.

Moreover, since these sociologists assume that racial prejudice in the North might be reduced by enriched experience, education, or therapy, they focus their attention on the social structure of the South and eschew any comparative analysis of the structures in both regions. Even when they turn their attention to black-white relations in the North they disregard concepts like caste in favor of less obdurate-sounding terms such as "job ceiling," "class differences," and "mobility patterns."

In general, the concentration on the Southern pattern of racial order was justified because at the time these studies were undertaken the vast majority of blacks lived in the South and because the codification of racial control was far more apparent in the South than elsewhere. Nevertheless, the sociologists thereby missed an opportunity to study more subtle patterns of race relations and to uncover the complex and diverse versions of institutionalized racism that exist outside the South. Certainly the central features of a caste order—prohibition on intermarriage, segregation, and "untouchability"—are also found in other regions.

If, following Gerald D. Berreman, we define a caste system as a hierarchy of endogamous divisions in which membership is hereditary and permanent,[35] then elements of caste will be found throughout the United States. Legal prohibitions on marriage between whites and blacks at one time existed in twenty states outside the South,[36] so racial endogamy has by no means been exclusive to that region. In addition, schools, churches, and occupations in the North have been organized, whether formally or informally, around ideals of white supremacy. Finally, it is at least worth a sociological supposition that in the North white-black relationships are characterized by set expectations of racial etiquette and by strict limitations on intimacy.

Studies of black ghettos in the North demonstrate the existence of caste without admitting the concept into their analyses. St. Clair Drake and Horace R. Cayton's *Black Metropolis* documents the growth, organization, and social complexity of a black ghetto in Chicago. The separate black community is a white creation maintained by policies of exclusion and segregation. Intermarriage in Chicago is feared by whites; it is the most significant reason for their refusal to admit blacks to their clubs, cliques, and churches.[37] A "color line" bars association of blacks and whites in a host of intimate institutional settings. Occupational advancement is by no means uniformly facilitated by membership in labor unions, and blacks feel the necessity of maintaining their own racial solidarity in order to secure benefits. While blacks and whites mingle freely in public places, they do not frequently enter into intimate associations with each other.

That blacks would harbor resentment at their position and develop an ambivalent orientation toward their self-worth seems just as inevitable in Chicago as it is in "Southerntown." Perhaps the mental anguish is even greater in the North, since there, unlike in the South, the trappings of the open, mobile society that exist almost exclusively for whites are ideologically professed to be available to all Americans.

In a more recent study in the North, conducted in a rural Connecticut town, elements of caste order have also been found, although here there is a greater admixture of countercaste elements and a smaller proportion of blacks in the community.[38] Connecticut does not appear to have had an antimiscegenation statue,[39] but intermarriage is infrequent and social relations between the races are not usually intimate. In the public schools there are a few reports of white girls dancing with black boys, but mixed dating is said to be a source of annoyance to whites and not encouraged by blacks since it might outrage public opinion.

Residential segregation is a definite feature of the town, and most of the community's blacks inhabit a rundown section near the railroad tracks and an iron foundry. Restrictive covenants prevent blacks from moving out of the ghetto. They are employed primarily in the town's iron foundry, but none have progressed to the rank of supervisor or into certain specialized types of work. Explanations of their concentration in this work do not indicate discrimination; but lack of skills, paternalistic management, and images of black undependability limit their occupational advancement. Some blacks are hired in a shirt factory, but none are employed in the town's public utilities, banks, bars, or specialty shops or in any of its professional offices. Public facilities are officially open to all, but occasional incidents of hostility and discrimination are reported. Blacks are not active in the political organizations of the town.

In "Connecticut Town" there are techniques of control which maintain the pattern of compliance to the social order by blacks. Whites rarely employ violence against blacks, but the fear of it is sufficient to keep blacks from moving into white neighborhoods. Blacks are also "kept in their place" by direct insults and refusals of service, especially in real estate transactions, job applications, and bars and taverns. Economic pressure, legalistic measures, or paternalistic connivance may be employed to further dependency among the blacks.

Black activities in "Connecticut Town" can be interpreted as a pattern of adjusted response to their domination by white society. Generally blacks avoid contacts with whites and thereby reduce opportunities for embarrassment or angry encounters. Experiences of rebuff by whites add to the avoidance pattern. The net result is a lack of aggressiveness with respect to changes in status: There is a conspicuous absence of any local black organization seeking greater rights and opportunities.

Historical studies also suggest that American society has had caste features in sections other than the South. Leon F. Litwack's study of the free blacks during the slave era reveals that prejudice was a frequent feature of black-white relations in the North and that exclusion or segregation was established in schools, churches, occupations, and politics long before the post-Reconstruction era.[40] Eugene

H. Berwanger's analysis of anti-black prejudice in the American West indicates deep-seated hostilities, vicious attitudes, and discriminatory practices all along the expanding frontier.[41] Louis Ruchames has documented ideological and intellectual support for prejudice, segregation, and prohibitions on black opportunities in the years between the Colonial era and the Civil War among Northern scholars and leaders.[42] I. A. Newby has shown the literary, scientific, and sociological rationalizations for segregation and discrimination that characterized early-twentieth-century thought outside the South.[43] Eugene Genovese has suggested that a study of experiences of blacks in the North and a proper analysis of the historical evidence force the conclusion that the South has not had a monopoly on racism.[44]

It would seem then, in the light of all these researches, that a correct understanding of the black's position in America would emphasize not the distinction between racial prejudice and a racial caste system but that both prejudice and a caste system are features of a larger and prior phenomenon—racism, a value that arose at a particular time and became embedded in complex ways in the fabric of Western social organization.

Although Dollard and others help us to understand the persistence of a pattern of caste and segregation in the South, they fail to inform us of the origins of that pattern. Moreover, by distinguishing between racial prejudice and caste order they direct scholarly attention away from the recognition of racism and the search for its origin and institutionalization and toward separate and discrete studies of attitudes in the North and caste structure in the South.

Both theory and evidence would suggest an alternative approach. Critics of Aristotelian persuasion have suggested that sociologists might begin their researches with the assumption that patterns of social organization are relatively fixed. From this supposition they might regard all changes as breaks in the pattern and search for the antecedent factors that brought about the changes. Validation of these postulated change-causing elements might be made by comparative historical investigations of similar phenomena. Without going into all the problems in the philosophy of science raised by these observations, we might suggest that sociologists recognize that American social values have an origin in specific events, which, complex as they are, must be studied to discover just how current beliefs and practices came into existence.

Recent historical works throw light on the origins of racism. Winthrop Jordan has shown how the contacts of Europeans with Africans and Indians in the fifteenth, sixteenth, and seventeenth centuries raised fundamental questions about the nature of man and society and that the answers to these questions, not merely by scholars but by practical men of affairs, established racism as both a belief system and a set of practices maintaining social distance between the races.[45] A similar set of findings on early relations between Europeans, Indians, and Africans has been made by Thomas Gossett, who shows how in the later centuries various racial assumptions were reinforced by theoretical discoveries, popular ideologies, and literary themes.[46] Studies of relations between Indians and whites in Spanish America and in the New England colonies reveal the beginnings of racist practices and prejudicial stereotypes.[47] One can conclude, thus, that the caste order of the South and the racial patterns of the North are not modes of social organization which have their roots in human nature or in inevitable historical processes but are grounded in specific events—in acts by persons or the institutions they control.

Seen in this light, Dollard's and others' studies of American communities take on new significance. Their analyses of the persistence of racism can be combined with the studies of the origins of racism to form a more complete picture of American race relations and the peculiar position of the black man. Second, racial prejudice and caste may be viewed as two forms of the same phenomenon. With this in mind, sociologists might search for just those conditions which favor the emergence of one or the other form. Moreover, by perceiving racism as a value that has been institutionalized, sociologists can ferret out those practices, perhaps innocuous on their face, that play a part in continuing discriminatory conditions.

IV

GUNNAR MYRDAL'S *AN AMERICAN DILEMMA*

IN 1944 Harper and Brothers published the most monumental sociological study of the black American to date—*An American Dilemma*, the fruits of a mammoth interdisciplinary research project carried out under the sponsorship of the Carnegie Corporation and the general guidance of the Swedish social scientist Gunnar Myrdal.[1] Not since the comprehensive work by the distinguished (though largely forgotten) black historian George Washington Williams—*The History of the Negro in the United States*,[2] published in 1883—has such a compendium of data been made available.

In its 1,024 pages of text *An American Dilemma* includes sections on the nature of the black problem, population and migration, economics, politics, and justice; social inequality and social stratification; leadership and concerted action; and the black community. Moreover, the appendixes contain theoretical discussions of the place of values in social science, general aspects of sociological methodology, and a brief discussion of the place of women in American society, which Myrdal saw as a parallel to the race problem. In no other single work will the student of race relations find so much information carefully compiled, clearly presented, and cogently organized. It is not our intention to review the study in all its complexity; it is with the basic theory, fundamental assumptions, and sociological imagination that informed Myrdal's researches that this chapter will be concerned.

An American Dilemma includes a critique of sociological thought on the race question, a value theory of the origins of racial prejudice and institutionalized racism, and an argument that the "American Creed" is antithetical to racial prejudice.

To Myrdal the bulk of American sociological thought on the black man is characterized by a conservative, laissez-faire, and fatalistic bias.[3] He points to William Graham Sumner's Social Darwinism and his scientific interest in folkways and mores as two closely related tendencies inclining him to perceive society in terms of a static social order not easily amenable to social change. Despite the melioristic sociology of Lester Ward, which Myrdal thinks is less than clear in its methodological principles, American sociological thought came to be dominated by the theories of societal stability represented by Sumner.

Thus Myrdal observes that Robert E. Park, although much less conservative than Sumner, was "still bound by a similar fatalism," which found expression in Park's emphasis on "natural" forces as opposed to individual acts. Myrdal suggests that Park might have been deterred from a more activist conception of man by his "keen observation of social conditions—and, perhaps, also some disillusions from his reform activities. . . . Not observing much in the way of conscious and organized planning in his contemporary America except that which was bungling and ineffective because it did not take due account of the natural forces, he built up a sociological system in terms of 'natural' causation and sequence." Park's writings reveal a "systematic tendency to ignore practically all possibilities of modifying—by conscious effort—the social effects of the natural forces." Their net effect, Myrdal concludes, is to encourage a "do-nothing," or laissez-faire, attitude about racial relations.[4]

Moreover, Myrdal argues, "Park's naturalistic and, therefore, fatalistic philosophy has been transmitted to some of his students who have been working on the Negro problem." For example, E. B. Reuter, whose works on the black American bear the stamp of the American conservative bias, speaks of man's relations to his environment in terms strikingly reminiscent of Darwinist ethological and ecological studies. "Whether we consider plants, animals, or human beings," Reuter writes, "we find that, in the large, they are in those areas where each is best fitted to thrive and prosper, and that each is somewhat nicely adapted in its structures and in its habit system to the special conditions of existence in the habitat. . . . Adaptation is the price of survival."[5]

Similarly, William F. Ogburn, although not a student of Park's, is cited by Myrdal for his observation that cultural lag is a social force against which man's efforts are futile:

> The process of keeping up with the pace set by technology may be slowed up because of the increasing heterogeneity of society and the possible greater number of institutional lags to be caught up. Therefore, no prospective integration of state and industry is expected to deliver us in the future from grave social disturbances.[6]

Finally, Myrdal is careful to point out that the Marxism that appears explicitly or implicitly in much of American sociological thought does not contradict its basic naturalistic and deterministic bias. The teleology implied in Marx's materialistic conception of history is, as Myrdal sees it, "of the do-nothing (laissez-faire) variety; that is, it is biased in the static and fatalistic direction." To the extent that American sociology adopts a Marxist perspective, Myrdal seems to be saying, it chooses that form of it that relies on history's inevitability rather than man's own efforts. Marx's forces of history are made to operate on man's fate in the same way as Sumner's folkways—as a deterrent to planned action and consciously guided social change. Indeed, Myrdal accuses Marx himself of this very bias:

In his principal writings Marx shows—contrary to what is often popularly assumed—no interest whatsoever in social planning. He expected "the reign of freedom" in the classless communistic society to arise full-fledged by natural force out of a political revolution caused by trends in technology and production. The interest in social reforms which he showed particularly in later days were a result of an ideological compromise.[7]

Thus, Myrdal charges, even in its adaptations from radical social thought American sociology shows a relatively inflexible commitment to naturalistic rather than humanistic orientations:

Social scientists are so habituated to using static and fatalistic value premises . . . that they often do not realize that it is quite possible to couple dynamic value premises with factual knowledge of mores, social processes, or social trends. The static and fatalistic value premises have actually imbedded themselves into the data. And it should not surprise us that the great development of social sciences in recent decades in America has not been accompanied by any correspondingly important development of social engineering.[8]

To counteract this kind of thinking, Myrdal proposes a dynamic conception of man and society that seeks to restore some balance of power between conscious design and historical and social forces. His conception of dynamic value premises centers attention not only on the content of the mores, folkways, and processes in society but also

on the desire to change them in accordance with some
purposefully sought goal:

> Recognizing the folkways and the mores, for ex-
> ample, and having a desire to *change some of them* in
> one direction or another, we should be interested in
> studying the range and degree of inertia; all the excep-
> tions to the folkways; the specialization of groups; the
> conflicts (between persons and within persons); the
> changes, the flexibilities, and the manageability of
> some factors in the social system; instead of, as Sumner
> usually does, stressing and exemplifying the great over-
> all inertia. On the practical plane we should make not
> only the negative inference that a plan for social change
> should expect to be time-consuming and to meet strong
> resistance, but also the positive inference that it has to
> direct its attack on certain points where the mores are
> weakest and where people are already beginning to
> question them (or have a divided conscience with
> respect to them). We should also infer that it should
> not attack them directly but should create situations
> where the people themselves will strain the mores.
> Similarly, if we recognize the tremendous force of
> certain processes and sequences we might, with a
> dynamic value premise, deduce that strategy demands a
> redirection or stoppage of processes which contain
> within themselves a motive power in a certain direc-
> tion, and an effort *against* individuals coming to adjust
> themselves to the processes. Finally a recognition of
> the sweep of social trends and of the basic role of
> invention and economic organization in social causa-
> tion, coupled with a dynamic instead of static valua-
> tion, would lead one to facilitate the perfection and
> adoption of those inventions which have the greatest
> promise of moving the society in a desired direction
> and to seek *social* inventions which would modify

economic organization and the effects of mechanical inventions.[9]

Moreover, Myrdal extends his criticism to the very concepts employed in American sociology and suggests that the terminology itself conceals hidden value premises of a conservative and laissez-faire type. In discussing Sumner's conception of the folkways and mores, Myrdal writes:

We must voice our grave skepticism toward the simple explanatory scheme concerning the role of valuations in social life typified by William Graham Sumner's concepts "folkways" and "mores." Since his time these concepts—or one of their several synonyms—have been widely used by social scientists and have, in particular, determined the approach to the Negro problem. The formula will be found to be invoked with some regularity whenever an author expresses his attitude that changes will be slow, or, more particularly, that nothing practical can be done about a matter. It is closely related to a bias in social science against induced changes, and especially against all attempts to intervene in the social process by legislation. The concept of mores actually implies a whole social theory and an entire laissez-faire ("do-nothing") metaphysics, and is so utilized.

Leaving aside for the present the political connotations of Sumner's construction, and focusing our interest only on its usefulness as a scientific tool, our main criticism is the following: By stowing the commonly held valuations into the system of mores, conceived of as a homogeneous, unproblematic, fairly static, social entity, the investigator is likely to underestimate the actual difference between individuals and groups and the actual fluctuations and changes in time. He is also likely to lose sight entirely of the important facts, that even within a single individual valuations are operative on different planes of generality, that they are typically conflicting, and that behavior is regularly the outcome of a moral compromise. . . . If Sumner's construction is applied . . . it is likely to conceal more than to expose. It conceals what is most important in our society: the changes, the conflicts, the absence of static equilibria, the lability in all relations even when they are temporarily, though perhaps for decades, held at a standstill. The valuation spheres, in such a society as the American, more nearly resemble powder magazines than they do Sumner's concept of mores.[10]

For this same bias Myrdal attacks the concepts that underlie functionalist thought in sociology. Much of modern sociology, he contends, shows an uncritical acceptance of the natural-law philosophy set forth so naïvely during the Enlightenment. According to this view, "natural laws" are not only right but also, despite the foolish activities of governments out of harmony with nature, actually operative in society without need of legislation. It is believed that legislation, unless it accords with natural law, will be inefficacious and mildly counterproductive with respect to nature's inevitable course. Myrdal points out that sociological terms such as "balance," "harmony," "equilibrium," "adjustment," "accommodation," "function," "social process," and "cultural lag" carry with them the tendency to emphasize the "do-nothing" orientation.

Moreover, Myrdal notes, when situations are described as harmonious, in equilibrium, or composed of organized forces in a state of accommodation or adjustment to one another, it is inevitably implied that some sort of ideal has been achieved, that the common good is being served, and that further movement in such a direction is desirable. Opposed sociological terms such as "disharmony," "disequilibrium," "disorganization," and "maladjustment" describe undesirable situations and connote in general a negative evaluation.

> Similarly [Myrdal continues], if a thing has a "function" it is good or at least essential. The term "function" can have a meaning only in terms of a presumed purpose; if that purpose is left undefined, or implied to be in the "interest of society" which is not further defined, a considerable leeway for arbitrariness in practical implication is allowed but the main direction is given: a description of social institutions in terms of their functions must lead to a conservative teleology.[11]

Myrdal concludes that the conceptual framework of American social science allows bad situations to exist if these situations are represented in naturalistic terms, while it discourages all human intervention in social affairs unless that intervention is explicitly seen as in accordance with inevitable trends—in which case it would appear to be unnecessary anyway. "The use of such terms," Myrdal writes, "makes it appear that a given situation is desirable or inevitable without the explicit specification by the social scientist of what he considers desirable or of the possibilities of the modification of 'inevitability.' "[12]

In addition to making a plea for explicit values in social science, Myrdal also urges American social scientists to reexamine their own fundamental concepts to see whether they do not contain, as he argues, clandestine conservative values. More specifically, Myrdal insists that the observation of social facts is itself conditioned by either conscious or hidden value premises and that the study of facts alone cannot yield any conclusion about the goodness or desirability of the situation which those facts describe.

In light of Myrdal's spirited criticism of American sociological thought in general and the social scientific study of the black in particular, it is perhaps puzzling that Ralph Ellison, one of America's leading black writers and a scholar quite familiar with sociological writings, should have criticized him for committing many of the same errors, sharing most of the same biases, and generally misunderstanding black life in just the same manner as those very same sociologists. In a review of *An American Dilemma* written in 1944 but which did not come to light until two decades had passed, Ellison discusses Myrdal's work in terms of its sponsor's intentions, its essentially un-Marxist approach, and its failure to grasp the spirit of black life in America.[13] By focusing on Ellison's criticisms we may point up some of the crucial areas of Myrdal's work that subsequently require our own critical attention.

An American Dilemma was conceived by the Carnegie Corporation in 1937 and especially by one of its directors, Newton D. Baker, a Southerner, the son of a Confederate officer, a man educated in the South and one who had been heavily criticized by black groups when he served as Secretary of War in Woodrow Wilson's wartime cabinet. It is Ellison's contention that the entire survey was underwritten by a capitalist institution in order to find the correct techniques to employ so that a new and academically enlightened self-interest could exploit the human and material resources of the South. "*An American Dilemma,*" he wrote, "*is the blueprint for a more effective exploitation of the South's natural, industrial, and human resources.*"[14]

By "exploitation" Ellison means to include both its positive ("democratic and fruitful usage") and its negative ("more efficient and subtle manipulations of black and white relations") connotations. As Ellison sees it, the Carnegie Corporation engaged in a grand theatrical gesture: "The whole setting is dramatic. A young scholar-scientist of international reputation, a banker, economic advisor to the Swedish Government and a member of the Swedish

Senate, is invited by one of the wealthiest groups in the United States to come in and publicly air its soiled democratic linen."[15] However, although Ellison does not mention this fact, Myrdal was a Democratic Socialist more inclined to liberal pragmatism than doctrinaire Marxism.

As Ellison interprets Myrdal's dilemma, "In interpreting the results of this five-year study, Myrdal found it confirming many of the social and economic assumptions of the Left, and throughout the book he has felt it necessary to carry on a running battle with Marxism. Especially irritating to him has been the concept of class struggle and the economic motivation of anti-Negro prejudice which to an increasing number of Negro intellectuals correctly analyzes their situation."[16]

All this may be correct, of course. But the point Ellison fails to mention is that to Myrdal a narrow-range Marxism that emphasized the historical laws of the class struggle is *too conservative* a thesis to adopt. As we have shown, Myrdal favors a humanistic and dynamic theory of social change. In place of any single-factor causal theory, Myrdal proposes a theory of cumulative causation. In Myrdal's conception, every single facet of black life in America is assumed to be related to every other, so that a change in any one factor, it is assumed, will produce a change in every other factor in the same direction. However, the element of time is important with respect to change, because some factors, *e.g.,* education, produce their effects at a slower rate than others, *e.g.,* a rise in the employment of blacks. Moreover, counteractive forces and the irregular rate of positive accumulations slow down the process of cumulation. "The system regularly develops under a great multitude of different outside pushes, primarily directed against almost every single factor," Myrdal concludes. "The actual pushes go in both directions, thus often *turning the system around on its axis as it is rolling.*"[17]

Myrdal's model of social change for the black is, then,

one which assumes a slow and sometimes irregular process in the direction of a purposefully conceived goal once a single powerful push in the direction of that goal has been made.

> Ideally [Myrdal writes], the scientific solution of the Negro problem should thus be given in the form of an interconnected series of quantitative equations, describing the movement of the actual system under various influences. That this complete, quantitative and truly scientific solution is far beyond the horizon does not need to be pointed out. But in principle it is possible to execute, and it remains as the scientific ideal steering our endeavors.[18]

In the light of both Myrdal's criticism of his sociological predecessors and Ellison's "Marxist" criticism of Myrdal's study, it is necessary to inquire just how humanistic and dynamic the theory of *An American Dilemma* is.

In questioning just how far from his sociological forebears Myrdal has moved, it is worthwhile pointing out that although he objects to the hidden bias of evolutionary and functional concepts, the very concepts he employs are subject to the same accusation. Myrdal's model of society, though not explicitly organic, is characterized by those very same features which describe such a model. In an engaging touch of modernity, Myrdal employs "mechanical" terms such as "rolling," "axis," and "system." Each of these terms, however, carries with it the same tendency to emphasize a laissez-faire or gradualist approach as the concepts of the Social Darwinists. Moreover, a mechanical model carries with it the conservative connotations of equilibrium and friction, which are remarkably close to the more traditional organic concepts of American sociology, such as homeostasis and strain. Finally, the specific proposals which Myrdal makes with respect to ameliorating the condition of blacks emphasize a gradualist and cautious approach not notably different from that of his predecessors.

Our main criticism of *An American Dilemma*, then, is based on Myrdal's failure to depart from the heritage of assumption that has obfuscated earlier sociologists. He is as committed to a conception of vague but powerful social forces playing a predominant part in social organization as those predecessors whom he criticizes.[19] True, his is a "softer" determinism than Sumner's and of about the same consistency as Ward's. But Myrdal did not advocate an abandonment of the Aristotelian assumptions of classical American sociology, nor did he provide a new sociology rooted in free will or in man's inherent capacity to remake the world.

Myrdal's twin conceptions of a "soft" but definite determinism and a melioristic social engineering force him into postulating a single value system for American society. Although Myrdal promised formal and methodological discussions, he later pointed out that "time and space have . . . prevented the subsequent complementation of our results by applying alternative sets of value premises, except at a few points." But the main reason for not carrying out his methodological promise is that, as he himself says, "the selection of the instrumental norm [*i.e.*, the American Creed] *has* material significance" and that "the whole direction of our theoretical research actually becomes determined by this norm. We have given one particular set of valuations a strategically favorable position in the study." And, Myrdal continues, "Measured by the standards of our ideal for research and keeping in mind all other possible sets of value premises, it is a one-sidedness in approach, and we should be fully aware of it."[20]

Myrdal seems at times to be saying that the American Creed is just one set of values competing with others in a kind of pluralistic and Hobbesian societal pit. From this position he appears to adopt the fairly orthodox scientific move of taking a one-sided approach, employing the creed in a strategic way to highlight certain features of American society in general and race relations in particular. However, this is not his actual position at all.

For Myrdal the American Creed is *the* national ethos, a basic and dominant set of values which takes precedence over all others. Myrdal specifically rejects a pluralistic image of values and any conception of equal competition among values. Indeed, he states that "the Negro problem would be of a different nature," and that it would be "simpler to handle scientifically, if the moral conflict raged only between valuations held by different persons and groups of persons."[21] In fact, Myrdal insists, American society is characterized by a unified culture. Despite the nation's heterogeneity and "the swift succession of all sorts of changes in its component parts, and, as it often seems, in every conceivable direction," there is nevertheless a basic homogeneity and stability in its valuations. "Americans of all national origins, classes, regions, creeds, and colors have something in common: a social *ethos,* a political creed. It is difficult to avoid the judgment that this 'American Creed' is the cement in the structure of this great and disparate nation."[22]

Myrdal's assertion of a unified culture is absolutely necessary to his central thesis. A unified culture is perceived by Myrdal to be a system straining toward consistency. The American Creed is the common value set whose system-wide adoption would be the final fulfillment of that striving. Any condition short of total consistency creates a strain in the system which, though it might be temporarily resolved by such psychological techniques as rationalization and such social techniques as propaganda, must ultimately be solved by a commitment to full-fledged consistency in action and beliefs.

The racist beliefs and discriminatory practices in America

constitute contradictions to the American Creed. Myrdal does not treat this complex of beliefs and practices as a creed equal in strength to the doctrines of democracy, equality, and progress, which make up the fundamental American ethos. Rather, he regards them as highly particularistic and local and, more to the point, morally lower in the eyes of the American. Thus the American is caught in a deep personal moral conflict in choosing between the "higher" values of the American Creed and the basic attitudes of racism: "The American Negro problem is a problem in the heart of the American. It is there that the inter-racial tension has its focus. It is there that the decisive struggle goes on."

For Myrdal the conflict in the hearts of men is fundamental to the social change which he expects in American race relations:

> The moral dilemma of the American [is] the conflict between his moral valuations on various levels of consciousness and generality. The 'American Dilemma' . . . is the ever-raging conflict between, on the one hand, the valuations preserved on the general plane which we shall call the 'American Creed,' where the American thinks, talks, and acts under the influence of high national and Christian precepts, and, on the other hand, the valuations on specific planes of individual and group living, where personal and local interests; economic, social, and sexual jealousies; considerations of community prestige and conformity; group prejudice against particular persons or types of people; and all sorts of miscellaneous wants, impulses, and habits dominate his outlook.[23]

Myrdal is convinced that the social trend in America is toward the resolution of this moral conflict on the side of the American Creed. One reason for his belief is found in his general assumption that "higher" values generally win out in the long run over "lower" ones. A second reason is given in his assumption that societies in general always strive toward value consensus. Finally, he argues that the decline in popular theories of black inferiority, which his researches had uncovered, is evidence of this trend.

The entire body of Myrdal's argument is open to question.

First, it is perfectly possible in theory and reasonable on the basis of the evidence to postulate that racism is not a "lower" and "local" set of values but rather a complex value premise equal in every respect to that of the American Creed. Myrdal's original theoretical approach should have forced him to consider this at least *as a possibility*, since in his formal report on methods he explicitly enunciates the proposition of competing values. Moreover, the evidence presented in the report itself on the political, economic, social, sexual, and personal aspects of racism would seem to bear out such a hypothesis. Finally, in historical and cultural studies made since Myrdal completed his work—notably Winthrop Jordan's *White Over Black*[24]—there is ample evidence to suggest that racism and the Enlightenment philosophy emerged together as uneasy values operating in tandem on, and reinforced by, practices in Western culture.

Second, even if it is accepted that racism is a morally inferior value to most Americans, it is perfectly possible for a person to maintain contradictory beliefs without suffering excruciating pangs of conscience or seeking to bring his beliefs into line with logical consistency. F. Scott Fitzgerald once remarked that "the test of a first-rate intelligence is the ability to hold two opposed ideas in the mind at the same time, and still retain the ability to function."[25] Extensive empirical work suggests that precisely that quality of intelligence to which Fitzgerald referred exists among ordinary Americans.[26] Myrdal recog-

nizes the role of "rationalizations" and "compartmenta-
lization," but he insists that these are but uneasy and
temporary resistances to the inevitable development of
consistency in thought and action. Myrdal's teleology is
rooted partly in his own optimistic bias and partly in his
acceptance of the reality in America of his mechanical
model operating in cumulative and unidirectional motion.
Posed potentially against this model are several alternative
ones. A society rooted in social equilibrium, one in which
Americans continue to preach progress and practice discrimination with psychic impunity, is just such an alternative. Given America's long history of racism, this model
deserved consideration, but it did not receive any in
Myrdal's study.

Third, Myrdal's theory of value consistency in complex
societies stands in sharp contradiction to an alternative
theory of social complexity and normative pluralism.
Whereas Myrdal assumes that social change in America
moves in the direction of uniformity and consistency,
there is much evidence to support an opposite view.
American society may be conceived of as a pluralistic one
wherein there exists a multiplicity of identities and moral-
ities. In this perspective, general values—such as the American Creed—are less relevant than individual beliefs and
particular actions. Rather than fusing into a common value
system, American society would appear to be fraction-
alizing into groups sharing particular norms. Such a pluralistic society need not be racist—indeed, a plurality of
beliefs would suggest the possibility of some circles
wherein no such beliefs hold—but neither does it guarantee
the elimination of racism. Instead, a pluralistic society of
multiple norms suggests the possibility of a struggle for
value supremacy and social power. The outcome of such a
struggle is by no means clear, and thus the triumph of
egalitarianism and democracy is by no means assured. Such
a model of society precludes a teleology dictated either by

the inexorable strength of age-old traditions or by the promise of an inevitable unification of "higher" values. Instead, it suggests a sociology rooted in what Maurice Merleau-Ponty has called an "innerworldly humanism"[27]— that is, a sociology that focuses on man in a struggle against society, against other men, even against himself, in order to forge social edifices about which he can only have tentative hopes. Recent advances in philosophy[28] and a new wave of sociology[29] uphold the rectitude of this new image of man and this problematic and open-ended image of the world.

Finally, when we turn to Myrdal's proposals for amelioration of the race problem, we see just how a commitment to a unified value system and a mechanical equilibrium model generates cautious, slow, and gradualist policies. According to his theory of cumulative causation, a move to enhance civil rights in any single institutional arena will have positive effects in every other arena. However, since some institutional payoffs proceed at a more rapid rate than others, it is of the utmost importance to choose one's sphere of action strategically and speed the course of cumulative repercussions. Voting, according to Myrdal, is just such a strategic arena for effective action. Myrdal cites with apparent approval W. E. B. Du Bois' comment that "a disfranchised working class in modern industrial civilization is worse than helpless. It is a menace, not simply to itself, but to every other group in the community . . . it will be ignorant; it will be the plaything of mobs; and it will be insulted by caste restrictions."[30]

Myrdal goes on to point out how blacks need the franchise to protect themselves, and how many features of disfranchisement, such as poll taxes and literacy tests, are withering away. Moreover, he points to the growing stake the North has in the enfranchisement of Southern blacks.[31] Nevertheless, when he presents his "practical conclusions" on this subject Myrdal offers a program that is modest in scope and consciously gradualist, a program not likely either to antagonize white Southern conservatives or to provide ballot-box protection to that class of blacks most in need of it. Myrdal's conclusion is that "the Southern franchise situation, which on the surface looks so quiet, is highly unstable and that, indeed, *the Southern conservative position on Negro franchise is politically untenable for any length of time*." However, he believes that a "value premise" should be agreed upon concerning the speed of social change and that "changes should if possible not be made by sudden upheavals, but in gradual steps." On this basis he concludes that there is an "urgent interest, and actually a truly conservative one, for the South *to start enfranchising its Negro citizens as soon as possible."*[32]

Since Myrdal apparently concurs in the Southern white conservative's charge that many disfranchised blacks are unintelligent, unfamiliar with American institutions, and likely to be corrupted by possession of the most fundamental device of political power, the vote, he proposes a division of the black population into an enfranchisable group of "higher strata," who are to be granted the right to vote immediately, and of poorer and less educated classes, for whom the right to participate in the political process will be granted gradually, apparently in increments.[33] As Myrdal sees it, the choice is between a carefully guided movement of "cautious, foresighted reforms" or an uninformed, unintelligent development of "unexpected, tumultuous, haphazard breaks, with mounting discords and anxieties in its wake."[34] (Ironically, in his testament of hope for the former course he adopts a perspective largely at variance with his general sociological stance but remarkably close to an open-ended, problematic humanism similar to that of Merleau-Ponty. "Man is a free agent," Myrdal writes, "and there are no inevitabilities. All will depend upon the thinking done and the action taken in the region during the next decade or so. History can be made. It is not necessary to receive it as mere destiny."[35])

Myrdal's sociological image of society leads him into proposing programs of slow, orderly changes that will resonate harmoniously with the slowly changing social trends. Moreover, he postulates a homogeneous and uniform structure of values in American society, suffering only from strains created by local practices and consciously contradictory beliefs. Thus Myrdal is unable to imagine a particular identity or a special role for the black.

Blacks, in Myrdal's conception of them, do little more than respond to the negative features of American society; their responses are constrained and modified by their own unqualified acceptance of the American value system. Nowhere is this better illustrated than in Myrdal's idea of the "rank order of discrimination" held by whites and blacks. This famous paradigm—which has become one of the most discussed features of Myrdal's work[36]—purports to show that the white man is most concerned to prevent intermarriage and sexual intercourse among blacks and whites and, in descending order, is concerned over the breakdown of etiquette and the increase of intimate relationships, the desegregation of public facilities, schools, and churches, political disfranchisement, discrimination in law courts, by police, and other public servants, and—last and least—discrimination in securing land, credit, jobs, and welfare, whereas "the Negro's own rank order is just about parallel, but inverse, to that of the white man."[37]

Leaving aside the actual empirical validity of Myrdal's paradigm, it is testimony to a remarkable instance of cultural consensus. According to Myrdal, blacks and whites agree on the elements of the core culture but disagree only on their priorities. The idea of a separate black culture or a subculture developed in isolation is not taken seriously by Myrdal.

It was this failure even to hypothesize a separate and special phenomenon of black life in America that provoked one of the most serious objections from Ralph Ellison. Commenting on Myrdal's observation that "the Negro's entire life, and consequently, also his opinions on the Negro problem, are, in the main, to be considered as secondary reactions to more primary pressures from the side of the dominant white majority,"[38] Ellison asked, "But can a people (its faith in an idealized American Creed notwithstanding) live and develop for over three hundred years simply by *reacting?* Are American Negroes simply the creation of white men, or have they at least helped to create themselves out of what they found around them? Men have made a way of life in caves and upon cliffs, why cannot Negroes have made a life upon the horns of the white man's dilemma?"[39]

Ellison's objection corresponds to our own earlier criticism that Myrdal's fundamental sociological theory remains bound by the teleological determinism of his predecessors. It is precisely because of his adherence to a mechanical model, his insistence on a unified culture, and his emphasis on the uniformity of the American Creed that Myrdal is forced to reject the possibility of a special and unique black life in America in favor of relegating the black to his traditional image as representative of a problem in American life. Moreover, according to Myrdal, the black problem, despite its peculiar characteristics, is not unlike that of other groups, including poor whites[40] and women:[41] "The Negro problem is an integral part of, or a special phase of, the whole complex of problems in the larger American civilization. It cannot be treated in isolation."[42]

Myrdal contends that the entirety of black existence in America is dependent upon the general American culture. "There is no single side of the Negro problem," he writes, "whether it be the Negro's political status, the education he gets, his place in the labor market, his cultural and personality traits, or anything else—which is not predominantly determined by its total American setting."[43] Myrdal's failure here is one of theoretical perspective and sociological imagination. Given his postulation of a unified American culture, it was inevitable, perhaps, that Myrdal would include the black in it. And it would seem that this perspective inhibits the intellectual imagination from developing a different, or, to use Robert S. Lynd's fine phrase, more "outrageous,"[44] hypothesis.

A humanistic, nonteleological perspective might have induced Myrdal to ask how blacks perceived America, how they defined their situation, how they saw their past, present, and future, and how they went about making sense of their world. To be sure, Myrdal gives a special kind of answer to these questions, but it is an answer rooted in his idea of the psychology of response: Blacks are not permitted to exist on their own terms; black history is but a special part of American history; black personality is but a painful and sometimes pathological reaction to the oppression of whites.

Myrdal's theoretical perspective ultimately forces him to see blacks as Americans with black skins. Perhaps his is a correct perception. But blacks—more, it would seem, than any other minority—might have been given the benefit of the doubt with respect to a personal, creative, and independent existence. There should be justice and libertarianism in American sociological theory even if it does not exist in American society.

Conclusion

Gunnar Myrdal's theory of an American dilemma is, despite his disclaimers, another study in the tradition of classical American sociology. Devoted to depicting black life in America, Myrdal imprisons it within a single value culture to which it can respond only by ultimate assimilation. Convinced that both individuals and institutions are

subject to strain caused by the disparity between prejudicial actions and the public promise of equality, Myrdal
couches his optimism about the eventual solution to the
black problem in terms of his belief that such contradictions cannot for long be countenanced. Thus he exchanges
the teleology of the traditional mores of the past for the
teleology of a value-consistent psyche of the future. His
practical solutions are on the same order as those of his
conservative predecessors: slow, gradual steps consistent
with age-old beliefs, guided by intelligent benevolence, and
eschewing social tumult.

Myrdal sees the black as existing in the shadow of
American culture, dependent on its slow but inexorable
changes, subject to its cultural, social, and idiosyncratic
whims, to be liberated by eventual absorption into the
American system, which will then have triumphed in the
final solution to the black problem.

V

PSYCHOLOGICAL THEORIES OF RACE PREJUDICE: THE BLACK AS A VICTIM OF A WHITE PERSONALITY DISORDER

CLASSICAL sociology perceives the black as a subject of predetermined social forces. Robert E. Park systematically presented the stages through which the black would inevitably pass on the way to his eventual assimilation in a racially homogeneous world. John Dollard, exploring the conditions of blacks in a setting of precarious accommodation, documented the complex reciprocity that sustains the essentially inegalitarian situation. Gunnar Myrdal provided an analysis of the future of the black in terms of a system of contradictory values out of which would emerge a consistent moral order rooted in the "higher values" of the "American Creed."

The trend in these studies is that of an intellectual movement away from concern with the physical and cultural traits of the black and toward the psychological characteristics of American society in general and of white men in particular. Gordon Allport and T. W. Adorno and his associates carried this trend to its quintessential completion: They see the black, together with the Jew and other members of minorities, as the victim of white men's mental problems; only with the elimination of these mental problems will the race problem become soluble.

The problem with this approach is in its reductionism. The race-relations problem is viewed in terms of a negative mental set that some people have toward others. Problems of discrimination are subsumed under the problems of prejudice. Emphasis is placed on locating the source of prejudice in the person. While occasional acknowledgment is made of the social and structural settings in which racial prejudice occurs, the primary study is of the psychological background that predisposes a person to racial prejudice. The black has but a shadowy existence in such a perspective. His physical, social, historical, cultural, and personal reality is declared to be unknown and—until the clouds that blot out white men's perceptions are lifted—unknowable. Moreover, in certain cases the mental blindness is so total that it is an unlikely possibility that the person will ever be persuaded to a morally appropriate attitude toward black people.

The Nature of Prejudice

The leading psychological approach to the study of racial prejudice was developed by Gordon Allport (1897-1967). Allport favored a direct approach to the "compound" of racial prejudice. In a portentous comment directed toward his professional peers who held that his concept of prejudice was sloppy, value-laden, and not properly grounded in psychology, Allport compared the study of prejudice to that of mental illness:

Psychopathologists regard paranoia or neurosis as undesirable; but paranoia and neurosis as syndromes nevertheless exist. School teachers regard certain mental sets as objectionable; the mental sets are there. Whatever our values may be, prejudice is *a fact of mental organization* and *a mode of mental functioning*. It is our business to understand it.[1]

Prejudice, then, like psychopathology, is a recognized

state of mental affairs. Moreover, again like psychopathology, it is an undesirable state. Hence it follows that psychologists should study its manifest forms, discover its root causes, and provide cures for it.

Central to Allport's observations about prejudice is the idea of a system in balance. He conceived of systems existing at the several levels of human existence—the cultural, the social, and the personal. Furthermore, he took over into his conception a dual orientation toward equilibrium. Ideally, not only is each specific system in a state of balance with respect to its constituent elements, but the three systems correspond to one another in a kind of universal unity. Prejudice conceived of as a value orientation, then, could be studied at each systemic level, but this would require the reorienting of study into conformity with systems theory. Thus, Allport concluded on this point:

> A methodological paradox exists: prejudice (like other forms of social behavior) is many things; it is one thing. It may well be that the solution to this paradox lies . . . in revising psychological theory—let us say—so that it corresponds in every essential feature with cultural and social theory. Certainly in the long run quarrelsome differences have no place in the scientific analysis of a single form of social action.[2]

To Allport cultural and social theory meant systems theory—the ideas about a social and culture system in balance that had already germinated in Myrdal's conception of American society and that would find higher theoretical development in the work of Talcott Parsons and Clyde Kluckhohn.

How could psychological theory find a correspondence with this kind of thinking? One way would be to posit conceptions of man that correspond to conceptions of society and culture in a state of homeostasis. The ideal man in a state of psychic equilibrium is held out as a vague but powerful human ideal toward which men should aspire and toward the creation of which psychologists should direct their melioristic attention. Such a man is not constrained by cognitive distortions, emotional incapacities, or myopic perceptions. He understands reality, controls and uses his emotions in a positive manner, and sees clearly. Such a man is, among other things, not afflicted by prejudice, which, Allport believes, is a compound of cognitive errors and displaced hostilities.

Allport went further than most in attempting to describe the ideal: the "tolerant personality" who "makes no distinction of race, color, or creed. He not only endures but, in general, approves his fellow men."[3] Some tolerant persons, Allport notes, are hyperconscious of the necessity for fair play and are actively motivated toward achieving it; others "are so habitually democratic in their outlook that for them there is neither gentile nor Jew, neither bond nor free."[4] Some tolerant persons are such simply because they live in a community where ethnic issues do not arise; others are "character-conditioned" toward a positive view of all mankind. Some tolerant persons exhibit a militant intolerance of the intolerant; others maintain quiet and friendly convictions about man. Almost all tolerant persons are liberal in their political outlook, but some tolerant orientations appear in the radical perspective, beclouding a character that may be wholly negativistic and charged with hate. Tolerant people may be better educated, but the evidence here is by no means unambiguous. Tolerant people have a greater capacity for empathy than those who are intolerant and also seem to have greater insight. Finally, the tolerant person is inclusive and generous in his relationships. As Allport perceives it, tolerance is an organized total orientation: "Tolerant thinking about ethnic groups is, no less than prejudiced thinking, a reflection of a total style of cognitive operation."[5]

As with tolerance, prejudice manifests itself in degrees and varieties. But before we describe the prejudiced person there is the prior question: What is prejudice?

To Allport racial prejudice is "an avertive or hostile attitude toward a person who belongs to a group, simply because he belongs to that group, and is therefore presumed to have the objectionable qualities ascribed to the group."[6] It is a compound resulting from three fundamental mental processes: categorization, displacement, and rationalization.

Categorization, as it functions as part of the prejudice syndrome, consists in overgeneralization, a process of concept formation having little basis in knowledge or experience. While categorization in general appears to be a normal mental function, overgeneralization with respect to racial groups takes the form of creating or accepting stereotypes. Stereotyping consists of the imputing to members of a racial minority an overgeneralized attribute or constellation of attributes that have negative connotations. However, prejudices differ from misconceptions, which are judgments that appear to be of the same cognitive type, in one important respect: The former are not subject to change when exposed to contradictory information, while the latter are. Indeed, as Allport suggests, the prejudiced person shows considerable anxiety and erects emotional defenses when persons or events threaten to contradict his deeply ingrained racial beliefs.

Displacement occurs when the behavioral consequences of anxieties produced in a particular context spread over wider and irrelevant contexts. Just as limited knowledge sometimes produces a cognitive leap to overgeneralization, so a frustration arising out of a specific situation may irradiate a man's whole existence for the duration of its emotional charge. The displacement argument is, of course, a general application of the older thesis of frustration and aggression: Persons who are frustrated with respect to particular goals but who are inhibited by inner feelings or external codes from directing their anger at the actual target or cause of their frustration will direct hostile feelings or aggressive acts against irrelevant targets, such as minority groups, that happen to be eligible for a more generalized hostility.

Finally, rationalization takes over to justify the hostility expressed toward the racial group. Since open expressions of racial animosity are generally objectionable in American society (Myrdal's American Creed, to which Allport frequently alludes), racial slurs are often accompanied by "evidence" marshaled to justify the accusations. In addition to justifications rooted in "facts," there are forms of account-giving which condemn those who insist on a tolerant view, which differentiate the particular evildoers from the general class to which they belong, which absolve one's friends from the putative evil traits while holding the class to which they belong to be properly described, and which distinguish the individual member of a class from the class itself.[7]

Beyond rationalizations are two other devices by which individuals may resolve inner conflicts over their prejudices: repression and compromise. The former consists of a denial by the person that he is exhibiting racial prejudice, the latter of a partial resolution of the dilemma that divides his conscience from his actions by means of a complex rhetoric that admits the inconsistency but finds a suitable justification for it.

Because Allport views the prejudiced person from the point of view of the realizable ideal of an "integrated personality,"[8] he appears to regard these devices of rationalization, denial, and compromise as mildly pathological deviations from the ideal.

As in his discussion of the tolerant personality, Allport

also employs typification to define the prejudiced personality. He issues the important caveats that not all persons who exhibit prejudices are necessarily revealing a total orientation, that prejudices may be inhibited by sanctions, conformity to the American Creed, or inner controls, and that occasional acts of discrimination are a commonplace in America. However, just as there is a normatively ideal tolerant personality, so at the other end of the continuum there is a personality whose very essence is intolerance. For the characteristics of this type, Allport draws on the study carried out by T. W. Adorno and his associates in 1950, *The Authoritarian Personality*.[9]

As summarized by Allport, the characteristics of the intolerant or "authoritarian" personality are ambivalence toward parents, moralism, dichotomization, a need for definiteness, externalization of conflict, institutionalism, and authoritarianism. What is perhaps remarkable about these characteristics is that, taken alone, they have nothing whatever to do with ethnic matters. Allport recognizes this point but nevertheless concludes that it cannot be gainsaid that these characteristics are found in combination with strong anti-Jewish and anti-black sentiments. "Our picture may be oversharp and may later need modification and supplementation, but the basic fact is firmly established— prejudice is more than an incident in many lives; it is often lockstitched into the very fabric of personality."[10]

The Etiology of Prejudice

Allport's outlook on the causes of prejudice is ambiguous and difficult to state in precise terms. Wavering between social and psychological explanations of prejudice, he suggests a multidimensional approach to the study which would include six different levels of analysis—historical, sociocultural, situational, psychodynamic, phenomenological, and earned reputational. None of these approaches is complete in itself, he admits, but each throws valuable light on the subject:

> By far the best view to take toward this multiplicity of approaches is to admit them all. . . . We may lay it down as a general law applying to all social phenomena that *multiple causation* is invariably at work and nowhere is the law more clearly applicable than to prejudice.[11]

Allport's six approaches coincide with his conception of a unified systematic social science. The historical and sociocultural approaches represent the contributions of the disciplines studying collective human endeavor, and the latter four approaches constitute psychology's own multi-dimensional approach.

Allport's generous statements about the theories of prejudice should not blind us to the pivotal element in his own thinking, the concept around which he based nearly all his psychological efforts—the human personality. In an essay written in reply to his critics, Allport observed that for all the sociological arguments stressing the influence of the environment over personality, there must still exist the prior condition of the person:

> But here is the nub of the matter. No man would say anything at all, nor do anything at all, unless he harbored within himself—in his own personality—the appropriate habits, or expectancies, or mental sets, or attitudes—call them what you will. Some inner dispositions are causing him both to talk like an angel and act like a devil, or to talk like a devil and act like an angel. What else than this did Myrdal mean by "the American dilemma"? It is not only possible, but usual, for Americans to have within their personalities contrasting and conflicting attitudinal dispositions.[12]

In his discussions of the prejudiced personality, Allport actually distinguishes two types. In addition to the intolerant personality, Allport discusses the conformist who feels no real antipathy but rather behaves in a manner consistent with the mores of his community. In a community characterized by racial animosity, the conformist will exhibit appropriate signs of his acquiescence, but in a community marked by tolerant codes of conduct he will just as easily carry out his activities in tune with the prevailing social attitudes.[13] From the point of view of melioristic action, then, the conformist personality—who, by the way, is believed by Allport to be representative of as much as one-half of the American population[14]—presents no necessity for psychological treatment. Rather, his compliant nature suggests the need to apply social constraints and institutional changes to create a tolerant community in which he will happily conform.[15]

The prejudiced personality, on the other hand, presents a truly psychological problem. The origins of his hostilities are ultimately to be discovered in the frustrations he repressed at an early age. The displacement of these hostilities onto blacks, Jews, or other minorities becomes fixed in the later stages of his maturation when he learns that such groups are more eligible for his hostile feelings than, let us say, his parents. While all prejudice is learned (Allport specifically rejects an instinctual aversion "among species that are cross-fertile"),[16] presumably the preconditions for rigidity and excessive hostility are established in the early years of socialization and catalyzed by later learning.

A person, then, acquires his personality and thence his predisposition to prejudices, if any, in the course of early childhood. Allport distinguishes between cases of *adoption* of prejudices (conformity) and *development* of prejudices. The latter arises from a course of childhood training which, while it does not transfer ideas and attitudes directly to the child, creates an atmosphere in which he will develop prejudice. A home that is "suppressive, harsh, or critical—where the parents' word is law,"[17] is likely to predispose a child to prejudice.

Parents by dispensing or withholding love in an absolute and arbitrary manner force the child into hyperconscious and fearful anticipation of their disapproval. Further, the authoritarian parents mold the child's conception of reality so that he recognizes a world of domination and authority rather than equality and trust. Wishing to avoid parental sanctions, the child learns to fear and distrust his own impulses, since it is through their open expression that he earns his punishment. Finally, the child projects his fears and distrust onto others, especially strangers; he suspects them of having evil designs and forbidden aims.

In addition to the authoritarian home, Allport points to three other child-rearing styles that seem conducive to the development of prejudice: "Although we cannot yet be dogmatic about the matter, it seems very likely that rejective, neglectful, and inconsistent styles of training tend to lead to the development of prejudice."[18]

By contrast, permissive parents are likely to predispose a child toward tolerance:

> The child who feels secure and loved whatever he does, and who is treated not with a display of parental power (being punished usually through shaming rather than spanking), develops basic ideas of equality and trust. Not required to repress his own impulses, he is less likely to project them upon others, and less likely to develop suspicion, fear, and a hierarchical view of human relationships.[19]

In conformity with the basic pattern of a systems approach, Allport's conception of personality development is evolutionary. His evolutionism is quite sophisticated, however, implicitly perceiving the development of a tolerant or a neutral personality to be likely unless certain impediments—*e.g.*, an authoritarian home life—stand in the way. Moreover, basic to Allport's discussions of personality is the concept of the functional autonomy of modes of behavior. In origin, at least, such modes are purposeful; they have a goal or serve a function. Once established, however, they need no further stimulation.[20] Hence, once a mode of behavior has become firmly lodged in the personality it is extremely difficult to extricate.

Emphasizing his evolutionary view, Allport speaks of the "dawn of racial awareness" as the time in the age cycle when the child comes to link color with ethnicity and to attach moral judgments to this association, judgments usually clustered around his association of skin colors with cleanliness or dirt.[21] The next stage apparently consists of the child's learning to attach emotion-laden labels, terms which he has already heard and added to his vocabulary, to other groups. Thus children learn to conceive of blacks as "niggers," of Jews as "kikes," of Italians as "wops," and so on.

In the next stage the child comes to reject totally the bearers of such epithets and will ascribe to them no favorable characteristics whatever. This period of total rejection reaches its peak in the early years of puberty and then begins to decline, setting the scene for the final stage, differentiation. In this highly sophisticated and adult period, the prejudices are less total, room is made for exceptions, and the racial animosities are adjusted to or accommodated within the cultural context of the society. As Allport sums up his evolutionary view of the development of prejudice in the personality:

The child who is first learning adult categories of rejection is not able to make such gracious exceptions (as are exhibited in phrases such as "Some of my best friends are Jews"). It takes him the first six to eight years of his life to learn total rejection, and another six years or so to modify it. The actual adult creed in his culture is complex indeed. It allows for (and in many ways encourages) ethnocentrism. At the same time, one must give lip service to democracy and equality, or at least ascribe some good qualities to the minority group and somehow plausibly justify the remaining disapproval that one expresses. It takes the child well into adolescence to learn the peculiar double-talk appropriate to prejudice in a democracy.[22]

To summarize Allport's views on the origins of prejudice, it is important to note that although he acknowledges the necessity of multicausal, multidimensional, and multidisciplinary approaches, he attaches special importance to the development of predispositions to prejudice. Such predispositions are acquired in the course of the socialization process, wherein prejudices may be directly taught as part of the early cognitive learning or they may be "caught" as a consequence of a particularly harsh, neglectful, or inconsistent domestic atmosphere.

The acquisition of prejudices, Allport observes, is a slow process passing through stages of development. At any stage the process might be interrupted, terminated, or redirected toward a more tolerant orientation. However, once a mode of behavior becomes established it assumes functional autonomy and its removal is by no means easy. Predispositions toward a tolerant orientation are most likely to arise in permissive settings where love and trust rather than punishment and suspicion are the central characteristics of child rearing.

The Alleviation of Prejudice

Given his emphasis on prejudice as a complex constellation of psychic traits arising in the development of personality, it is not surprising that Allport finds that most programs designed to reduce group tensions are less than effective. Civil rights legislation has only an indirect effect on prejudice, although, he adds, in the long run continuous conformity to the law may serve to bring private conscience and attitudes into line with public practice.

Of the nongovernmental programs Allport is far less reassuring. Research on the methods and programs for the elimination of prejudice is inconclusive but appears less than promising. Formal educational programs seem to be more conducive to reducing unfavorable attitudes if they employ an indirect approach and do not specialize in the study of minority groups or place primary focus on prejudice. Informational programs—*i.e.,* those that present factual information about minorities—"do not necessarily alter either attitude or action"; moreover, their "gains, according to available research, seem slighter than those of other educational methods employed."[23]

Programs designed to increase contact with minority groups, Allport states, are at best ephemeral so long as they are carried on within a society that countenances discrimination, and they may have a deleterious effect if carried out among persons who are sharply differentiated by social class. Group retraining programs, consisting of various types of therapeutic activities designed to lead to a kind of "forced empathy," are limited because they "cannot be used with people who resist both the method and its objectives."[24] Finally, "there are grounds for doubting the effectiveness of mass propaganda as a device for controlling prejudices,"[25] and exhortations about brotherly love have but a slight effect.

Allport observes that, on theoretical grounds at least, individual psychotherapy is perhaps the best single approach to the elimination of racial prejudices, since "prejudice is often deeply embedded in the functioning of the entire personality."[26] Moreover, the stressful individual who seeks psychiatric aid is usually desirous of some kind of change in his orientation or functioning, and even if his desire for help is not consciously related to his ethnic attitudes, "still these attitudes may assume a salient role as the course of treatment progresses, and may conceivably be dissolved or restructured along with the patient's other fixed ways of looking at life." Even if psychotherapy is not undertaken, Allport points out, almost "any prolonged interview with a person concerning his personal problems is likely to uncover all major hostilities." In discussing his problems, "the patient often gains a new perspective. And if in the course of the treatment he discovers a more generally wholesome and constructive way of life, his prejudice may abate."[27]

Catharsis—an explosion of feeling followed by a purging of those anxieties that led to the feelings—sometimes occurs in therapy. Catharsis has a "quasi-curative effect," Allport writes, for it temporarily relieves tension and may prepare the individual for a more fundamental change of attitude. Catharsis alone, however, is not a guaranteed curative but only a preparatory step. A therapist must employ it with caution. Nevertheless, Allport notes that with "patience, skill, and luck [he] may then at the right moment guide the catharsis into constructive channels."[28]

For all its putative effects on racial prejudice, Allport perceives the fundamental limitations of psychotherapy. First, the frequency of attitudinal transformations under therapeutic treatment is unknown. Much more important, however, is his forthright statement about its general promise: "but even if this method proves to be the most effective of all methods—and because of its depth and interrelatedness with all portions of the personality, it should be—the proportion of the population reached will always be small."[29]

The Limits of Therapy

Allport's analysis of the limited effectiveness of therapy for alleviating racial prejudice points up one of the problems of psychological explanations for any social ill. Prejudice is not the only problem that has been traced to the individual and his inner states. At one time or another, war, crime, delinquency, divorce, and unemployment have been explained as problems arising out of dispositions lodged in the individual.

When dysfunctional mental states are not regarded as innate or genetic, they are usually conceived of as arising out of some malfunction in the socialization process. Postponed in their outward manifestation until adolescence or adulthood (or, in Freudian terms, lying below the surface in a prolonged "latency period"), these orientations arise to plague the individual long after their originating sources have been forgotten or rendered inoperative. Social problems are thus the consequence of errors committed by unwitting parents (and, according to some theories, abetted by unintentionally harmful peers) during the course of childhood.

Traditionally, promoters of such explanations for social problems have formulated rather weak and ineffective solutions for them. Most melioristic social scientists are committed to the principles of liberal democracy and thus are constrained against advocating the kind of curative program that the relentless logic of their own formulations requires. For example, if it is argued that a particular kind of child rearing is likely to affix racial prejudice in the personality in such a manner that to remove it "the whole pattern of life would have to be altered,"[30] then why not advocate just such an alteration? Why not propose that all persons desiring to become parents be required to submit themselves to the battery of tests employed in *The*

Authoritarian Personality? Those that score significantly high on the "authoritarian" scale might then be restricted from procreating or, in a more humane program, be required to relinquish child rearing to the state or to a private agency guaranteeing an appropriate mode of socialization.

Further, why not propose that all persons who are already rearing children be submitted to the same or related tests and those who show significant signs of authoritarianism, neglect, or inconsistency be required to show that they can and will mend their ways or, failing that, be required to give over their children to foster or adoptive parents or agencies that will ensure a psychologically proper upbringing?

If indeed socialization practices are at the root of racial prejudice, and if, as Allport reports, research "suggests that perhaps 80 percent of the American people harbor ethnic prejudice of some type and in some appreciable degree" while only "20 percent of the people are, in Gandhi's terms, 'equiminded' or completely democratic in all their attitudes,"[31] then such drastic programs might seem both necessary and proper in order to eliminate racial prejudice and to reinvigorate democracy.

Of course, no American psychologist has proposed such a solution. A wholesale psychological examination of the American population on a compulsory basis, a reaching of the heavy hand of the state into the heart of every man, smacks of the very despotism that opponents of the prejudiced personality are so eager to prevent.

Thus the proponents of personality-rooted causes for social problems are caught in a terrible dilemma—and one of their own making. On the one hand, they are fairly sure that social problems in general, and racial prejudices in particular, are problems of personality disorder that can be traced back to errors in the learning process in early socialization. On the other hand, these same social scientists are for the most part liberal democrats, and therefore they cannot propose—indeed it may have never occurred to them to propose—a solution that would be absolutely triumphant over racial prejudice if that solution runs counter to democratic principles. In their attempts to resolve this dilemma they advocate changes that would check the symptoms of the problem (*e.g.*, legislation, which, while it does not immediately change the hearts and minds of men, at least alters their behavior) and propose, albeit with some realistic skepticism, voluntary programs (*e.g.*, educational and therapeutic sessions) in which at least some of the afflicted might be cured.

But so long as racial prejudice is explained as arising from prior personality states, and so long as social scientists remain attached to principles of liberal democracy, this dilemma will trouble the minds of all those dedicated to solving America's major social problem.

A Sociological Critique

Not all social scientists agree on the personality-rooted explanations of racial prejudice proposed by Allport, nor do they find themselves troubled by the "democratic dilemma" to which that formulation leads. Although there have been many criticisms of the attempts to link together sociology and psychiatry[32] and of the general personality theory of racial prejudice proposed by Allport and his associates[33] and a veritable avalanche of discussion of *The Authoritarian Personality*,[34] we shall confine ourselves to a summary of that able critique offered by Herbert Blumer in his address delivered at the dedication of the Robert E. Park Building at Fisk University in March, 1955.[35]

Blumer's critique offers a redefinition of prejudice, an explanation for its origin and persistence, and an implicit program for its dissolution. Moreover, in both his etiological formulation and his programmatic suggestions, Blumer avoids the paralyzing dilemma to which Allport's and others' formulations seem to lead so inexorably.

Blumer begins by specifically rejecting those formulations that perceive racial prejudice as a feeling or set of feelings lodged within an individual. Instead, he proposes that racial prejudice be viewed "fundamentally [as] a matter of relationship between racial groups." An individual perceives that he and others belong to specific racial groups and that the different groups occupy a complex hierarchy of positions vis-à-vis his own group. A person's identification of his own racial classification and that of others is a product of his experiences and his interpretations of them and, as such, is quite variable.

The process by which racial prejudice is formed, Blumer contends, is a collective one, in which a body of sentiments becomes crystallized into racial identities. Although the process is by no means fully understood, it appears to operate through the public media: Individuals acting as spokesmen for their own racial group publicly characterize another racial group in such a way as to place it in an opposed social position to their own group. "It is the *sense of social position* emerging from this collective process of characterization," Blumer concludes, "which provides the basis of race prejudice."

Although Blumer avoids speaking in such terms, he clearly perceives the process by which races become characterized as, in the broad sense of the term, a political one, for the very capacity to influence public images is a function of power. He points out that the origin of any particular sense of group position is to be found in the history of the relations between the groups. And immediately he conceives of these relations as being unequal: "Prestige, power, possession of skill, numbers, original self-conceptions, aims, designs and opportunities are a few of the factors that may fashion the original sense of group position." Depending on subsequent experiences between the groups. Blumer continues, the original sense of group position may become weakened or entrenched, socially more significant or less relevant, sharpened or dulled in its focus. In short, in their experiences with one another the groups fashion, modify, and reshape their social positions. Nevertheless, Blumer insists, the characterization of group position is a function of power relations. "However variable its particular career, the sense of group position is clearly formed by a running process in which the dominant racial group is led to define and redefine the subordinate racial group and the relations between them."

Characterization of a subordinate group is a product of interaction between members of the dominant group: "Leaders, prestige bearers, officials, group agents, dominant individuals and ordinary laymen present to one another characterizations of the subordinate group and express their feelings and ideas on the relations." There may be much inconsistency, contradiction, and varying states of intensity of feeling in these interactions, and while the parties may run against one another they may also stimulate and reciprocally intensify one another's views, producing a new emergent pattern. New currents of thought provide anchor points for definition. "If the interaction becomes increasingly circular and reinforcing, devoid of serious inner opposition, such currents grow, fuse and become strengthened. It is through such a process that a collective image of the subordinate group is formed and a sense of group position is set."

Moreover, Blumer observes, the collective image of the group is abstract. The group is defined as if it were a homogeneous whole: "While actual encounters are with individuals, the picture formed of the racial group is necessarily of a vast entity which spreads out far beyond such individuals and transcends experience with such individuals."

More specifically, Blumer denies that the images of race

that constitute racial prejudices derive from individual experiences: "The collective image of the abstract group grows up not by generalizing from experiences gained in close, first-hand contacts but through the transcending characterizations that are made of the group as an entity." Hence the arena in which racial prejudice arises is not that microcosmic one composed of individuals interacting in a local context but rather the public arena, "wherein the spokesmen appear as representatives and agents of the dominant group." Legislatures, public meetings, and the mass media are institutions in which the sense of group position is forged and reinforced: "The major influence in public discussion is exercised by individuals and groups who have the public ear and who are felt to have standing, prestige, authority and power." In addition, the powerful interest groups in any society may seek to influence the images formed of racial groups in order to serve their own particular interests. In short, Blumer shows that racial prejudice is a political product.

Another implication of Blumer's formulation is that the racial definitions that prevail in a society arise out of matters that are of crucial social and political significance. "The happening that seems momentous, that touches deep sentiments, that seems to raise fundamental questions about relations, and that awakens strong feelings of identification with one's racial group is the kind of event that is central in the formation of the racial image." Concluding this statement, Blumer points to the kind of episode that is likely to produce a particularly pejorative imagery: "When [a] public discussion takes the form of a denunciation of the subordinate racial group, signifying that it is unfit and a threat, the discussion becomes particularly potent in shaping the sense of social position."

But what are the properties of racial prejudice? According to Blumer there are four basic types of feeling that always seem to be present in a prejudiced sense of racial group position: a feeling of superiority; a feeling that the subordinate race is intrinsically different and alien; a sense of proprietary claim to certain areas of privilege and to certain advantages; a fear and suspicion that the subordinate race harbors designs on the prerogatives of the dominant race. These four feelings constitute a general orientation about the propriety of social positions. The first three represent a collective sense of what ought to be in the properly organized society, while the fourth exhibits a vague but powerful suspicion that social propriety is threatened by subversion.

The sense of group position is a norm and an imperative: "It guides, incites, cows, and coerces," Blumer asserts. With respect to it individuals are likely to have a variety of feelings ranging from the bitter and hostile to the polite and considerate. However, to the extent that they consider themselves as belonging to a dominant racial group, "they will automatically come under the influence of the sense of position held by the group." This may not be noticed when racial matters are placid, but if "the sense of position is strong, to act contrary to it is to risk a feeling of self-alienation and to face the possibility of ostracism."

Blumer concludes on this point: "The locus of race prejudice is not in the area of individual feeling but in the definition of the respective positions of the racial groups." But the sense of racial group position does not represent the sum total of feelings toward members of the subordinate race:

> The sense of group position refers to the position of group to group, not to that of individual to individual. Thus, *vis-à-vis* the subordinate racial group, the unlettered individual with low status in the dominant racial group has a sense of group position common to that of the elite of his group. By virtue of sharing this sense of position such an individual, despite his low status, feels

that members of the subordinate group, however distinguished and accomplished, are somehow inferior, alien, and properly restricted in the area of claims.

Racial prejudice, as Blumer notes, is a defensive device protecting the proprietary claims of the dominant racial group against the claims of "ineligible" racial groups.

How can racial prejudice be obviated from society? Blumer believes that the extent of racial prejudice is linked to how deep-rooted the idea of social position is in the social order. Hence in the South it is greater than in the North, where the social order is less affected by the sense of group position held by the dominant racial group. In the North racial prejudice has had a more variable and intermittent career, arising in a pronounced fashion only when disorganizing events arouse anxieties of the dominant group in response to a threat to its sense of group position. Beyond this observation Blumer suggests the social conditions under which racial prejudice is likely to recede:

The sense of group position dissolves and race prejudice declines when the process of running definition does not keep abreast of major shifts in the social order. When events touching on relations are not treated as "big events" and hence do not set crucial issues in the arena of public discussion; or when the elite leaders or spokesmen do not define such big events vehemently or adversely; or where they define them in the direction of racial harmony; or when there is a paucity of strong interest groups seeking to build up a strong adverse image for special advantage—under such conditions the sense of group position recedes and race prejudice declines.

Blumer's analysis of ways to decrease or eliminate racial

prejudice is limited and perhaps conservative. But from his approach other programs of a more direct and liberal kind may be derived. For example, it follows from Blumer's argument that, since racial prejudice is a product of characterizations of racial groups made by elites in the dominant group, opponents of racial prejudice might try to influence the elites that shape public opinion, particularly that element that helps reinforce the sense of group position in times of racial tension.

Blumer's essentially political analysis of the origins and nature of racial prejudice is couched in terms of a relatively static society in which the dominant group retains its position of power. However, his general sociological position invites analysis of a more dynamic kind. Thus blacks might seek to alter the entire structure of domination and subordination so that they no longer occupy an inferior position. Political movements in support of a black's candidacy for office, of voter-registration drives, and of black representation in the full range of occupations today controlled by discriminatory labor unions are examples of this kind of social action. In terms of Blumer's analysis, it is critical that the moves made by the subordinate race do not arouse such fear and anxiety in the dominant group that its spokesmen develop a countermovement of considerable strength.

Conclusion

Can Blumer's and Allport's positions be related to each other? Perhaps. Allport's analysis of racial prejudice is a study of the *private* sphere of social relations, far removed from the spheres of power and public-opinion formation that concern Blumer.

What is the relationship between the two spheres of human action? One answer would be that activities in the public sphere promote idiosyncratic behavior in the private sphere. For many years sociologists have been aware of the function of private arenas for the carrying out of strange, exotic, or deviant behavior.

If events in the public arena move in the direction of eliminating racial prejudice as an approved public stance, presumably overt racial animosity will be cast into the realm of idiosyncrasy or deviancy. But suppose that at the same time as racial prejudice is declining the private spheres are also shrinking, as a result of the extension of laws and mores into areas previously held to be in the private arena. It would then appear that the opportunities for the expression of idiosyncratic ideas would decline, possibly at a rate too rapid for many individuals' psychic absorption.

Programs that extend the rights and protections of the Constitution and the Bill of Rights to all Americans regardless of race are likely to arouse discontent and anger in those persons who derive a psychic benefit from racial prejudice and who need to preserve a territory for idiosyncratic action. The frustrations over such an enclosure of the private sphere and the types of action which it permits might engender an aggressive hostility among people for whom these idiosyncratic acts serve a function, because for them the expression of racial animosity is a necessary part of life itself.

In time, perhaps, these frustrations may subside as new objects for aggression arise or as the original animosity becomes extinguished because of disuse. In the confrontation between the prejudiced personalities and the harbingers of an enlightened and prejudice-free society we might at first expect considerable unrest, discontent, and manifest hostility, but in the long run the enlightened elites would win out and establish the prejudice-free society which would reflect their own tolerant values.

VI

THE SOCIAL SYSTEM AND THE BLACK AMERICAN: THE SOCIOLOGICAL PERSPECTIVE OF TALCOTT PARSONS

TALCOTT PARSONS provides one of the most thoroughgoing theories of racial prejudice, combining the psychological theories of Freud and Gordon Allport with a systems theory whose general outline was presented by Gunnar Myrdal.[1] Whereas Allport concentrated on the role of socialization in producing a predisposition to prejudice and Myrdal insisted on the efficacious role of the American Creed in resolving ambivalence on the race question, Parsons points to the structures in Western society that make frustrations endemic and aggressions inevitable.

The net conclusion to be drawn from Parsons' approach is that hostility toward some object or group in general, and very likely racial prejudice in particular, will be a central feature of Western society so long as it retains its basic social structures. However, Parsons argues, systemic evolution will eventually incorporate the black man into the dominant community.

The Functional Theory of Prejudice

As Parsons perceives it, the two institutions that in their ordinary operation are likely to produce those anxieties and insecurities that engender frustration are the family and the occupational system. The familial organization and the methods of child rearing in America are such as to produce emotional difficulties for all who are subject to them. The degree to which these difficulties are experienced, the ways in which they are resolved, and the forms in which they manifest themselves in behavior vary, but the ordinary member of society is bound to experience some sense of insecurity or anxiety as he grows to maturity.

Parsons argues that the setting of the American family within the society at large is conducive to rather high levels of insecurity for the child, especially for a boy. Because the conjugal unit is relatively isolated from larger kin groupings, the child is oriented toward a very small number of persons and primarily dependent for affection on his mother. As a result, children become highly sensitized to the nuances of emotional change in their mothers, apprehensive over any real or imagined loss of love from them, and jealous of the affection that mothers give their husbands.

In addition, Parsons observes, the child's need for love is not alleviated by associations outside the home. There he is placed in competition with his peers for approval from teachers, other parents, and adults in general on the basis of individual performances.

Moreover, because the general value system emphasizes individual achievement, the mother may give or withhold love on the basis of the performances of the child rather than out of any sense of unconditional affection. Love, then, becomes a very valuable but precarious element in the child's world. Parsons concludes on this point: "The situation is favorable to a high level of anxiety and hence of aggression. But because of the very acuteness of the need for affection and approval, direct expression of aggression is more than normally dangerous and hence likely to be repressed."[2]

Beyond these sources of frustration, Parsons continues, are the special ones that affect the different sexes more or less acutely. Boys are at a disadvantage since fathers are absent from the home during the day and thus the child is largely deprived of the "visibility" of a male role model because of his lack of direct contact with his father's workaday world. Boys, then, are vulnerable to the formation of a feminine identification because of the high degree of visibility of their mothers. However, this feminine identity is officially proscribed and, as the boy soon realizes, incapable of ratification since he cannot grow up to be an adult woman. In addition, boys learn from their peers, parents, and the mass media that women are inferior to men and that they ought to feel ashamed or guilty about any identification they have with this lower order of humanity.

Typically, boys experience this complex issue in early adolescence as a compulsive need to demonstrate their masculinity. Society assists them in this by its provision of masculine identity pegs in athletics, while youthful subcultures emphasize toughness of character and strongly depreciate any expression of tenderness or other "feminine" emotions. Nevertheless, Parsons states, these societal aids are not sufficient to prevent a deep-seated ambivalence about sexual identity and a gnawing fear that one's masculinity is not proved. Neurotic and psychotic disorders are often characterized by "mother fixations," and aggressive orientations toward women, who are blamed for the trouble in the first place, are quite common. However, since one's mother is not quite eligible for open hostility, such animosities must be repressed. This in turn causes still more frustration and displacement of aggression onto other targets.

A final source of frustration for boys, Parsons writes, is their orientation toward "goodness" or "badness." To the young boy the mother provides the model for good behavior by giving him signs of approval or disappointment with respect to his activities. Hence, when the boy revolts against identification with his mother, he unconsciously identifies goodness with femininity and may assume a positive orientation toward mischief.

Because this identification of goodness with femininity may be generalized and diffused over all the aspects of the culture identified with women, the boy's hostility will be equally pervasive. Parsons points out that "there is a strong tendency for boyish behavior to run in anti-social if not directly destructive directions, in striking contrast to that of pre-adolescent girls."[3] Moreover, since the entire "bad boy" syndrome is deeply embedded in the culture, mothers are apt secretly or unconsciously to identify with its expression, thus blessing their son's revolt at the same time that they are the targets of it.

However, the "bad boy" orientation is not suitable for adult masculine life. Adult males gain status according to their mental abilities and sense of responsibility, not the physical prowess and irresponsibility associated with youthful exhibitions of masculinity. Hence boys, just as they are finding outlets for their aggressions in "manly" efforts of strength and bravado, must begin to repress these forms of "healthy" aggression in order to move toward the next stage of masculine adulthood. The repression of boyish masculinity in adult males, Parsons contends, is probably "one important source of a reservoir of latent aggression susceptible of mobilization in group antagonisms, and particularly war, because it legitimizes physical aggression as such."[4]

Although the family system operates quite differently for girls, it is no less conducive to the engendering of frustrations. Female childhood may be less provocative of repressions because, while a boy is denied the day-long presence of his father, the maternal presence provides the daughter with a direct opportunity to learn the role of housewife and mother firsthand. However, Parsons notes, when she reaches marriageable age a girl must enter a highly competitive arena of her peers in order to "catch" the principal source of her future status and security—a husband. The competition is severely anxiety-provoking, since she is more or less alone in her situation of mate selection and since young men may not be entirely rational in their responses to her.

Parsons sees the free choice of mate that characterizes American marriage as likely to engender deep-seated ambivalence, a high degree of emotionality, and a low level of calculated rationality among marriageable young people. Moreover, a girl must contend—although she is often in no way prepared to do so—with the hedonic attitude toward sex which manifests itself at this time in young men as an aggressive response to their own repressed sexual orientation toward their mothers. While boys may seek sexual relations with the girls they date, they also tend to idealize a "good" woman in strikingly asexual terms. Hence girls seeking a mate must steer a careful course between promiscuous availability and puritanical refusal. The ambiguity of their role is a source of ambivalence in orientation, and they are constrained to repress actual feelings and inhibit specific actions. Hence frustrations and anxieties are sure to arise.

For the maturing girl there are two fundamental sources of frustration. First, there is her discovery that she, like all of her sex peers, is dependent on men for her security. In contrast to the secure situation of her childhood, when her mother was the center of attention and the model for emulation, the adolescent girl is shocked by the inferiority and dependency that adulthood promises. Second, the qualities and ideals which she absorbed in her childhood identification with her mother suddenly turn out to have little utility in solving her immediate problems and may become a definite liability with respect to competing for a suitor. As Parsons sees it, "The severity and relative abruptness of this transition cannot but, in a large proportion of cases, be a source of much insecurity, hence the source of a high level of anxiety and of aggressive impulses."

Women sense that they have been deceived by the very people in whom they placed their trust and affection—their parents—who falsely led them to believe that strict adherence to the maternal style is the way to security. The resultant aggression is directed against women, the primary deceivers, but also against men, because they have forced this insecure and inferior status upon women. A woman experiences insecurity over the apparently contradictory roles of glamor girl, sex partner, wife, and mother, and this in turn generates further anxieties and aggressions.

Parsons has summed up the general conclusions to be drawn about the aggressions endemic to the family system by emphasizing their tendency to be diffused and eventually displaced onto targets other than their original sources:

> The typical Western individual—apart from any special constitutional predispositions—has been through an experience, in the process of growing to adulthood, which involved emotional strains of such severity as to produce an adult personality with a large reservoir of aggressive disposition. Secondly, the bulk of aggression generated from this source must in the nature of the case remain repressed. In spite of the disquieting amount of actual disruption of family solidarity, and quarrelling and bickering even where families are not broken up, the social norms enjoining mutual affection among family members, especially respectful affection toward parents and love between spouses, are very powerful. Where such a large reservoir of repressed aggression exists but cannot be directly expressed, it tends to become "free-floating" and to be susceptible of mobilization against various kinds of scapegoats outside the immediate situation of its genesis.[5]

Moreover, Parsons shows, the direction of this displaced aggression is by no means unpredictable. Although he does not specifically point to blacks as the most likely target, the themes of grievance which these aggressions generate make them a very likely choice. The fact that men must assume sober responsibility and repress the adolescent cult of masculinity to which they aspire lends itself to revolts against the obligations of adulthood, reactions against the rights of others, and a refusal to treat women with tender affection.

In this context it is easy to see how blacks become the objects of fear, envy, and contempt. Imputed to be sexually superior to white men and secretly attractive to white women, relieved of all need to adopt the sobriety of adult responsibility, and assumed to behave in terms of their physical prowess, blacks represent everything that the white adult has left behind in adolescence, everything that the culture holds to be a sign of immaturity when evidenced in grown men, everything that the white man seeks to return to in his moments of fantasy and nostalgia.

Uncomfortable with their ambivalent emotions, white men seek to justify their choices by resorting to available racial categories. To the whites can be attributed all those elements that are officially praised and credited: Whites are the builders of "civilization," they assume the serious responsibilities of adulthood in society. Included here are the sacrifices of self and sexuality which they see as necessary to the creation and maintenance of civilization. To the blacks may be attributed the vices of savagery, the *machismo* of unrestrained physical prowess, and the promiscuity and sexual freedom of uninhibited eroticism.

Having made these distinctions between the races, whites will not only openly despise blacks but also secretly envy them. And this forbidden envy of a despised and pariah people is itself repressed, so that ultimately the hatred of them is compounded. The very existence of blacks reminds whites of their lost youth, while at the same time it threatens the civilization they built at the cost of giving up that youth. Thus blacks become the objects of displaced aggression.

In a more specific sense, the peculiar orientation of women to men may heighten men's frustrations and increase their aggressive and prejudicial feelings. A woman's subtle but real hostility toward the man with whom she is associated may evoke the compulsive masculinity which adult men are compelled to repress. However, a woman's ambivalent orientation toward men may take the form of idealizing precisely those qualities of manhood— masculinity, heroics, physical aggression, toughness—that must be inhibited, or at least only cautiously expressed.

Caught in an ambiguous situation, an adult man discovers that he must both exhibit and curtail those aspects of male identity which he associates with adolescence. The frustrations that develop therefrom are peculiarly suited to find expression in hostility toward blacks. Representative of uninhibited masculinity, of uncontrolled sexuality, and, in the fantasies of Western pseudoanthropology, of savagery, the black's very existence is a challenge and a threat to white men.

In Herbert Blumer's sense of racial group position blacks are conceived to be *below* the standards of white adulthood, *beyond* the chains of constrictive Western civilization, and yet to *have desires* on the social prerogatives and sexual property of white men. Moreover, as Parsons' argument would suggest, by their very state of "natural freedom" blacks are presumably more attractive to white women, who secretly admire precisely those masculine and savage traits which blacks possess by "nature" and which whites have sacrificed for civilization and status.

Only by becoming "white Negroes," to use Norman Mailer's felicitous phrase[6] —*i.e.,* by divesting themselves of culture and social station and assuming the lowly status and licentious sensuality of "niggers"—can whites ultimately thwart this assault on their sexual property. And since most whites are unwilling or unable to do this, Parsons' argument (which, incidentally, antedated Mailer's by several years and did not use the phrase "white Negro") runs, they instead continue to hold blacks in contempt, keep them in a distant and innocuous position, and secretly envy them their putative liberty. Racial prejudice, then, is a very likely outcome of the personal and social strains imposed by the structural basis of Western civilization—the family.

According to Parsons, the family is not the only source of frustrations. The occupational system, with its modes of recruitment and its function of conferring status, also engenders anxieties in all who accept its values and hence must weather its rigors.

The fact that the occupational system is the principal institution by which status is conferred stamps it with crucial importance. Not only the job holder but also his wife and children enjoy the status provided by his occupation. An adult is aware that his whole life, not only in the world of work but also his family, friendships, and recreation, is severely modified by the occupation he enters and by his particular location in that occupation's hierarchy of positions.

Parsons points out that the occupational world places primary emphasis on individual achievement. Employees are selected on the basis of their capacity to perform relevant tasks, on their innate ability, training, educational attainments, and demonstrated experience. Because the job places individual adequacy in the forefront of identity issues, the employee is constantly subject to the possibility of being found wanting in ability. This anxiety is heightened by the competition he faces once he embarks on the career journey. Competitiveness always holds out the possibility of losing, and while winning the contest undoubtedly provides ego security because it ratifies one's self-evaluation, the system operates so as to produce a considerable number of losers.

Because the rules of selection and advancement are based on achievement, an individual is foreclosed from explaining away his failures by reference to his birth or racial origins. The result is that feelings of inadequacy are endemic to the occupational culture, that exculpating accounts designed to rid oneself of feelings of personal failure are not likely to be efficacious, and that anxiety over performances is not casily assuagcd.

Moreover, Parsons continues, a man's work is likely to be both physically and socially segregated from the other spheres of his life and to be governed by separate rules and relationships. Tasks are often narrowly specialized and very exacting, and stress is often compounded by the essential orientations that govern the world of work—objectivity in judgments, inhibition of impulses, and strict rationality in action.

Several types of anxiety flow from this one condition. First, the inhibition of impulses at work tends to create a reservoir of unspent psychic energy which cannot be retained or repressed. This emotional reservoir frequently overflows at home, where it is "taken out" on wife and children and thereby creates anxieties for these victims of the occupational system. The constant dampening down of the emotions may also create an uneasy separation between the technical and the personal self, a breach which widens over the years. This dissociation of self is experienced as a division between the "real" and the required aspects of existence and engenders a frustrating desire to break out of this double-sided existence into a condition of "wholeness."

Second, the emotional complexity of the system of work relationships is not matched by permissible expressions at work, thus imposing additional strains on the individual, who must adhere to neutral and objective standards at all times.

Finally, because it is built upon a system of mobility, occupational status is inherently insecure. Employees are constantly having to readjust to new positions, new relationships, new apparatus, and the vicissitudes of the general economy. Adjustment to one stable situation is ruled out in principle except for those who opt to withdraw or deviate from the central value system.

Although all these considerations apply primarily to men, Parsons adds that women are also adversely affected by the occupational system. Although they are not directly involved, wives frequently bear the burden of emotional anxieties generated by their husbands' occupational strains. Moreover, as persons who must depend on reflected status, derived from activities in which they cannot participate, women experience a sense of frustration at being unable to control their own fate. And finally, because they are excluded from the arena where "big things" happen, women are once more reminded of their inferior status and are likely to resent the arbitrary system which condemns their sex to a dependent and largely impotent role. However, as wives and mothers they may not be able to engage in direct expression of these feelings, and repression and displacement onto more eligible targets may result.

Parsons' final comments on the sources of aggression emphasize that "it is above all in the occupational sphere that the primary institutionalization of the basic themes of the above discussion takes place—childhood is an apprenticeship for the final test which the adult world imposes on man."[7]

Since the ability to perform well, hold one's own, and excel in competition is a fundamental challenge of adult life, Parsons continues, most men are condemned to experiencing some sense of inadequacy. Moreover, many will feel they have been treated unjustly, cheated by fate or the system, or thwarted by elements outside their control. This sense of having been treated wrongfully, however, can serve as both a balm to resentment and an "acceptable" account for one's own failure: Success has been denied a good man because he was not given the opportunity to reveal his talents.

With respect to the channeling of aggression—that is, the displacement of aggression from the primary to a secondary target—Parsons' conclusions are pessimistic in the extreme. He suggests that there is no reason to suppose that, on the average, the absolute levels of frustration in the Western world will be lowered. There are few direct but innocuous outlets for the expression of aggression, so the general "need" for functional equivalents of the primary targets—*i.e.,* scapegoats—will remain at the same high level. Then, it would follow, even if blacks should decline in utility as "acceptable" scapegoats, society would still need their "moral equivalent" against whom to vent its accumulated aggressive energy. But, Parsons concludes, minorities are not likely to decline in their functional importance:

> On the one hand the peoples of Western society are highly susceptible to wishful and distorted beliefs in their own superiority to others . . . since this belief, and its recognition by others, tends to allay anxiety about their own adequacy. On the other hand, since such a belief in superiority has compulsive characteristics, those who have to deal with such people find it "hard to take," even when the former have a highly realistic attitude. But it also stimulates a vicious circle of resentment on the part of those who, sharing the same hypersensitivity, are treated as inferior. It is, in other words, inordinately easy for either individual or group relationships in the Western world to become defined

as relations of superiority and inferiority and to evoke aggressive responses if the assumption of superiority is, even justly, questioned, or if, again even justly, there is any imputation of inferiority.[8]

Writing in 1947, Parsons had in mind the vicious anti-Semitism of the Nazi era, but his description of the basic features necessary for a people to become a target for aggression can with only slight modification apply to blacks:

The "out-group" should . . . be a group in relation to which one's own group can feel a comfortably self-righteous sense of superiority and at the same time a group which can be plausibly accused of arrogating to itself an illegitimate superiority of its own. Correspondingly, it should be a group with a strong claim to a position of high ethical standing of its own which, however, can plausibly be made out to be essentially specious and to conceal a subtle deception. The Jews have in both these connections furnished almost the ideal scapegoat throughout the Western world.[9]

Following this logic, it might be added that, since they too have asserted a claim to a high and ancient African and Afro-American culture, blacks bid fair to replace Jews in the unfortunate position of the ideal scapegoat.

It is perhaps surprising to find that Parsons has been labeled as a conservative by his critics.[10] His psychosocial explanation of prejudice goes far beyond that of Allport, who, it must be remembered, perceived the prejudiced personality to be a consequence of particular kinds of child socialization. Parsons, while not stating that racial prejudice is the only pattern of aggressive response, does argue that a high degree of frustration and aggression is endemic to the West and suggests that ethnic group conflict is a very likely outcome of this condition. What he does not state explicitly, but what does seem to follow logically from his etiological analysis, is that the only sure way to end racial animosities and other pernicious antagonisms in the Western world is to completely revise the social system.

Perhaps because Parsons does not espouse revolution, because his general sociology is couched in terms of a society retaining its equilibrium while adjusting to sudden changes, and because he does not employ a Marxist analysis, his sociology has not been seized upon by revolutionaries or by radical sociologists. Nevertheless, it seems clear that his arguments could lead to the logic that revolution is the only solution to the race issue. In a projection of Parsons' sociology, such a revolution would presumably espouse a value and institutional system that would not engender frustrations, that would channel aggressions into constructive outlets, and that would provide an unambiguous surrogate for the black and other targets for aggression.

The Future of the Black in the Social System

In Parsons' later discussions of the prospects for blacks in America, there is no mention of revolutionary change.[11] Rather, in line with Myrdal's conception of a social system moving in accordance with its own dynamic, Parsons perceives American society as about to embark on the final phase of what he terms the "inclusion process" of the black minority. A revolution is neither necessary nor likely, since the conditions for remedying America's greatest social evil are at hand. Parsons holds that revolutions are likely to arise when the society is in fundamental conflict with the government, and, apparently, he foresees no such conflict. Moreover, he seems to be saying that any possible cause for social upheaval—in this case the festering frustration of blacks over their centuries-long exclusion from full citizenship—can be forestalled by bringing blacks into the mainstream of society.

Inclusion, as Parsons defines it, is specifically distinguished from assimilation because it permits survival of the ethnic community within a pluralistic society. Inclusion occurs in a three-stage process through which a group is gradually but steadily extended the full complement of citizenship. The first stage is the legal one, by which each individual is secured in his rights of person, property, religion, speech, association, and assembly as guaranteed in the Bill of Rights. In the case of blacks, the constitutional basis for civil rights constitutes the single most important lever upon which their implementation can be pressed. Because Americans are generally committed to granting these rights to all citizens, blacks may more easily make demands for civil rights than for the other two components of complete citizenship, political and social rights. Indeed, according to Parsons, it is these civil rights that are bound up in and to which an appeal can be made in behalf of what Myrdal has called the American Creed.

The second stage is political. By this Parsons means to designate not only the franchise by which individuals are given a voice in the selection of their leaders but also group participation for collective goals. Specifically, he has in mind the employment of lobbies for special group interests, the organization of voting blocs, and the institutionalization of politically effective assemblies for presenting petitions and demands to the government and the public. Political inclusion means being a relevant part of the party structure and not just during election campaigns. It means having access to the mass media to propagandize one's position, represent group needs, and espouse social causes. Parsons points to this crucial aspect of political inclusion: "The body of citizens needs 'spokesmen,' the potential influencer needs media for making his wishes and their gratifications known, and leaders need structural outlets for their opinions, appeals and proposals."[12]

The third stage is social and concerns not so much having the opportunity to exercise one's rights as it does having the resources to implement them fully. Most important here is access to the basic prerequisites for success in the society—in this case, to education and to the complete occupational spectrum. Parsons points out that the mere abolition of discrimination in opportunities may be an empty gesture devoid of any real promise if remediable handicaps still exist in the minority group and if these handicaps are linked to that group's status position. Social inclusion therefore requires the equalization of opportunity.

It is the third stage that Parsons believes is most significant for blacks. It involves two categories of resources. The first is economic. Individuals cannot take advantage of available opportunities unless they are in a financial position to do so. Parsons seems to suggest that it is the government's responsibility to ensure the financial capability of its disadvantaged citizens, for he points out that it was this "aspect of the social citizenship complex [that] was paramount in the discussions and measures of public policy during the New Deal."[13]

The second category of resources is related to the effective functioning of individuals and their families in the environment in which they find themselves—more specifically, this includes health and education. Parsons finds cause for optimism in the fact that "increasing attention is being placed on education as the most decisive link between the individual's underlying levels of capacity and his relation to the opportunity structure"[14] and in the recognition, presumably by the government, "that at the bottom of the social scale (as judged by the usual criteria of success, prestige, and so on) there is a vicious circle of cumulative *disadvantage*, which becomes accentuated the

more marked the 'competitiveness' of the society becomes."[15] Parsons concludes by pointing up the relevance
of these observations for blacks: "It almost goes without saying that the Negro in this country is very deeply caught up in this vicious circle and that . . . social
citizenship is particularly important in the present context."[16]

Parsons conceives of the stages of inclusion in an evolutionary schema. In true Aristotelian fashion he turns to the
origins of the United States, "the first new nation,"[17] to
discover the direction it would take in its unfolding
development.

The United States consolidated its nationhood with a
struggle for political independence, Parsons' argument
begins. The national "core" was white, Anglo-Saxon, and
Protestant. However, the fact that Catholics and Jews were
also included in the national makeup, that Protestantism
was both liberal and humane, as well as being factionalized
into denominations and sects, that Anglicanism could not
be established as a national church because of its association with the colonial power of England, and that the
Enlightenment ideology, assuring individuals of their rights
independent of their social status, was a pervasive influence guaranteed that inclusion of minorities would be the
eventual outcome of political and social development.

But if complete citizenship for all inhabitants was foreordained in the establishment of the new nation, Parsons
continues, that process was also predestined to be slow and
orderly because of built-in constraints against the adoption
of universalist norms. The fact that the United States is a
federal union gives individual states the chance to protect
particularist prerogatives and thus served to secure
slavery in the South until the passage of the Thirteenth
Amendment. The net result of federalism has been to limit
drastically the extent to which universalist principles could
be applied to minorities.

The unfolding of universal equality has been made possible by the slow but steady extensions of the Fourteenth Amendment to overrule state-protected particularisms and by the division of labor resulting from industrial development, immigration, and territorial expansion. However, Parsons notes, as private enterprise came to control the economy it tended to estrange business from government and to encourage suspicion of government in the private sector. This, in turn, militated against popular support for government action in behalf of blacks. On the other hand, the steady growth of industrialization and urbanization favored the subversion of particularist enclaves of opportunity and privilege. Though territorial expansion encouraged a uniformity in citizenship, the idea of regional interests promised that special ideologies, like that of the South, would be protected.

The fulfillment of the promise of American life requires a lengthy period of time and, Parsons points out, the unfolding of several collateral processes. Civic equality was embodied in the Bill of Rights but its implementation required years, during which state and local particularisms were allowed to erode at their own pace. The Civil War marked the greatest crisis of national solidarity, and in its aftermath there succeeded a traditionalist counterrevolt which restored antebellum values in the South. Moreover, the social welfare aspects of citizenship did not even begin to be recognized until the New Deal.

Within this general process of expanding citizenship, Parsons' argument runs, the several racial and economic groups proceeded at a pace dictated in great part by the degree to which they already possessed capacities that qualified them for civic inclusion and the extent to which they aroused anxieties among the general citizenry. Various peoples may, because of their own peculiar characteristics or because of the kind of imputations against them, evoke fears about their "foreignness," such as anxieties over the possibility that they will subvert or take over cherished institutions or that their inclusion will debase the quality of citizenship.

It would appear that despite their long history in the United States, blacks have not been eligible for inclusion until the present time; they now possess many of the necessary qualifications and are ready to begin the slow process of advancement into the civic, political, and social mainstream. As Parsons sees it, blacks have had to wait their turn behind other groups—European immigrants, Catholics, and Jews—who possessed the wherewithal for more rapid inclusion, but now that it is time for them to be included the process should proceed with all deliberate speed.

Parsons' argument is that all minorities eventually come to be included in the American societal community but that some proceed more rapidly than others because of the accidents of place, culture, and collective strength. In the case of the blacks, "both because of slavery and because of Southern regional isolation [they were] long kept insulated from the forces favoring inclusion."[18] However, Catholics and Jews, despite their late arrival in America and the xenophobic fears they aroused, proceeded through the stages of the inclusion cycle sooner than blacks.

It is beyond the scope of the present work to delineate Parsons' detailed description of the inclusion process for Jews and Catholics. Suffice it to say that, as Parsons sees it, neither Jews nor Catholics had to pass through the civic and political stages of the citizenship cycle; each had only to overcome onerous social exclusion and public fears about foreignness and subversion. And this was made easier by increasing urbanization and the diffusion of Jews and Catholics into the general population. Moreover, while Jews and Catholics seemed to move into and accept the public culture, whose pattern had been set by white Anglo-Saxon Protestants, they were not seriously hindered in the preservation of their ethnic identity in the private sphere, since religious pluralism has always been an accepted American value.

While European white groups seem to be exempted from the first two stages of the citizenship cycle, blacks must pass through all three. Moreover, blacks must overcome the widespread fear that their inclusion in the society on an equal and fully participating basis would sully the quality of citizenship itself. This fear is not only a product of prejudice, it also arises from the harsh fact that blacks, now at the bottom of the social and economic scale, do not possess the basic resources—capital, education, health, stable families—with which they could effectively utilize political rights and occupational openings to obtain further social rights. Finally, black ethnicity is rooted in race and culture, unlike that of Jews or Catholics, which is rooted in religion, and thus it does not enjoy the same prestige as that of a religious body. Nevertheless, Parsons believes, inclusion of blacks is a very likely prospect in the immediate future: "It is reasonable to suggest that, whatever the extent and nature of the responsibility for the many previous failures, the time is ripe for a major advance."[19]

But why has it taken so long for the inclusion process to affect blacks? Part of the answer is contained in Parsons' conception of the stages of citizenship. During the entire period of slavery blacks were excluded from even the most elementary aspects of citizenship. After the abortive Reconstruction period, the return of "home rule" to white Southerners and the concentration of blacks in the agricultural South foreclosed their opportunities for civic, political, or social inclusion.

With blacks living in isolation from the main currents in American society, other groups, notably Europeans from southern and eastern portions of that continent, Jews and Catholics, monopolized the attention of the makers of public policy. It was only after the migration of blacks out of the rural South into industrialized urban areas that the stage was set for the citizenship cycle to apply to black Americans. Myrdal's *American Dilemma*, completed in 1944, heralded the fact that blacks were for the first time in a position to begin the journey into citizenship, to pass through the successive stages of civic, political, and eventual social inclusion in American society.

Parsons also explains why there is a gap in time between the settlement of blacks in cities, a process well established by 1945, and the beginnings of the movement for black citizenship—why, that is, that the American Creed, which Myrdal had done so much to fashion into an instrument of public policy, did not begin to become effective until the 1960's.

Timing and salience account for the lapse. The continuous erosion of regional and ethnic solidarities by industrialization and urbanization, the development of a greater sense of interdependence and pluralism among Americans, the recognition of public responsibility for the maintenance of welfare programs, the emancipation of more and more victims of an inequitable system by the courts, and the urban migration of blacks established the necessary, but not the sufficient, conditions for ushering in the citizenship cycle.

For the conditions to be sufficient for the cycle to begin there would have to be a clearing away of other issues that occupy moral, social, and political attention. As Parsons puts it, "American society is not only complex and changing, but also pluralistic in a manner making it impossible for many—even (or especially) very vital—problems to be in the forefront of public attention and generalized political action at any one time."[20] Thus the civil rights movement could not emerge until the Great Depression, World War II, the Cold War, the Korean War, and the internal crisis of McCarthyism had passed off center stage.

Parsons asserts that the 1954 Supreme Court decision was the first major break. Then the events at Little Rock dramatized not only Southern resistance but also federal passivity. After that the election of a liberal Democratic administration in 1960 caused expectations to mount rapidly. But even this was not enough:

Indeed, the emergence of the problem into prominence, even on this level, seems to have depended, in addition to its inherent pressure for attention, on *two* independent sets of circumstances. First, there developed at least a temporary easing of the political tensions resulting from the new American position in the world power system—tensions which, except for the brief period of the early New Deal, had long inhibited domestic reform. Second, a new post-war generation, impatient with the cautious conservatism typified by Eisenhower, began to press for a program of active change. The election of Kennedy in 1960 was certainly a turning point. The moral sentiments, particularly strong among the activists of the younger group of both races, began to have effect.[21]

But, like Park's race-relations cycle, which would terminate in assimilation unless something interfered, Parsons' citizenship cycle may also be halted for a time. Parsons' evolutionism[22] bears close resemblance to that of Park. "Accidents" of history may interfere with the inclusion cycle's natural development—for example, the conditions which made possible the emergence of the civil rights movement as the central issue of the 1960's may change as the Vietnam War or the college rebellion challenges its salience. Even more important, Parsons adds, is the balanced mobilization of four categories of factors favoring integration. Should there be an imbalance in blacks' commitment to becoming full citizens, in the articulation of the basic direction of the movement for their inclusion, in the correct blending of the moral ideals of acceptance and the mobilization of political and business interests, or in the supportive role of the economic elements (upgrading of employment) of civic and social gains, then the cycle of citizenship might be slowed down considerably. On balance, Parsons does not believe these "accidents" will occur, but they might if the inclusion cycle is handled precipitantly:

> The process under discussion here is that of a major extension of full membership in the societal community. If it is done imprudently—as, it might be said, was the completely free immigration before World War I—it may have effects analogous to inflation. But the fears of it are just as irrational as the fears of economic modernization have been, and they can be analyzed in closely parallel terms. The most important single condition of avoiding inflationary "debasement" is the general upgrading not only of the Negro but of all elements in the population falling below the minimum acceptable standards of full citizenship.[23]

One of the most likely interferences with the citizenship cycle is the emergence of black nationalism. Since full inclusion of all elements of the population is the only solution "tolerable from the American point of view," Parsons writes, black separatists must not be permitted to gain active support in the black community. The vexing question of black identity and group solidarity is not insoluble. Parsons reminds us that inclusion is not the same as assimilation:

> My own view is that the healthiest line of development will be not only the preservation, but the actual building up, of the solidarity of the Negro

community and the sense that being a Negro has positive value. In the process there is the danger of cultivating separatism. . . . But the pluralistic solution, which has been stressed throughout this discussion, is neither one of separatism—with or without equality— nor of assimilation, but one of full participation combined with the preservation of identity.[24]

Thus Parsons' evolutionary solution to the black problem depends as much on a set of events ("accidents") not occurring as it does on the development of appropriate conditions and liberal policies. But Parsons is optimistic:

The process of social change which characterizes this type of society is not "total revolution," but focus on one or a few salient "problems" at any one time. The status of the Negro American is probably *the* salient internal problem of this period in our history. The prospects for its relatively satisfactory resolution depend on a combination of factors. Not least among these are the pluralistic institutional frameworks of the society, which make such processes of change procedurally possible with quite limited violent overturn, and the moral values characterized by Myrdal as the American Creed.[25]

Conclusion

In the work of Talcott Parsons we find a synthesis of all the previous writers we have discussed: His theory of social amelioration for the black contains all the promise and most of the faults of these earlier sociologists.

Like Park's race-relations cycle, Parsons' citizenship cycle is evolutionary and teleological. It projects a predetermined drama of black improvement which will unfold unless, like unbidden actors who steal the show with a forbidden entrance, certain developments interfere. Thus, in this view, events that contribute to the cycle are natural and preferred; those that interfere are unnatural and opposed.

If Parsons' cycle materializes as predicted, then social science is vindicated and the black becomes a full citizen; if it does not, social science is still vindicated, since accidents will have interfered with natural developments, and, as the time for teleological redemption is ever long, blacks may still have hope.

Finally, Parsons argues, all the adverse events that make up the history of blacks in America are obstacles that only temporarily blocked the natural trend of history. Man is thus perceived as a creature of forces ultimately beyond his control: He must acquiesce to the laws of evolutionary development or succumb before their inexorable force. If one rejects a deterministic world, however, then Parsons' entire construction falls in the face of man perceived as master of his own destiny.

VII

TOWARD A SOCIOLOGY
OF THE BLACK AMERICAN

THE thesis of this book can be stated simply: The sociology of the black man has not yet begun. Despite more than a century of study, blacks remain a sociological puzzle. The principal reason for this failure of a major discipline to deliver what it had promised is that American sociological thought has been dominated by a progressively more complex version of Aristotle's view that all things change according to principles of slow, orderly, and continuous motion. Modification of the original Aristotelian view has only added a more cumbersome sociological apparatus to support what should have been recognized as a moribund idea.

Although an alternative theoretical focus to that of Aristotle does exist, sociologists thus far appear reluctant to adapt it to the study of black life. Those sociologists who do reject theories of progressive and melioristic change within an evolutionary process tend to lose interest in the theoretical aspects of the study of the black altogether and to concentrate instead on immediate social problems, the psychology of prejudice, or the exhortative actions necessary to remedy the social evil of discrimination.

In view of recent and remarkable changes in the position and prospects of blacks, perhaps sociologists will re-examine their assumptions about the laws of social change and human nature and begin afresh with a new sociology of the black man and his institutions.

Classical American sociology did not adopt a rigorous approach to the sociology of race relations but rather subsumed the subject of race development under the rubric of evolutionist and especially Social Darwinist theories. Social anthropologists of this stripe undertook to locate blacks in the chain of human evolution, and sociologists accounted for contemporary racial problems and the alleged peculiar aspects of black behavior in terms of biological factors.

Social Darwinism spun off both conservative and liberal theories of human development. Conservative writers emphasized the racial struggle for survival. The more ethnocentric of these asserted that the white race had already attained victory in this struggle and urged that it be designated by science as the fittest of the races. A definite challenge to the prevailing biological ideas about race, conservative Social Darwinism did take into account the cultures of the several races, the social bases of behavior, and the multiplicity of society, but it also raised and failed to resolve numerous questions of evidence and suffered from an embarrassing form of tautological reasoning. Liberal Social Darwinists emphasized that the evolutionary cycle is *as yet incomplete* and predicted a raceless world as the ultimate outcome. In the interim, with respect to current issues of race conflict and assimilation, they favored specific programs to aid in social amelioration and promote positive evolutionary development.

The evolutionist theories of the Social Darwinists and the perception of the black as a "problem" interfering with the otherwise smooth development of American society are both elements of a larger set of ideas that did not receive systematic formulation until Robert E. Park developed his race-relations cycle. In constructing this cycle, Park adapted Aristotle's conceptions of science and social change to the study of race relations. For Aristotle a science could only study things that change according to

natural motion—that is, motion directed toward an unambiguous and predetermined end and occurring in a steady
and orderly manner.

These ideas had already provided the foundation for the
widely used "comparative method" of nineteenth-century
evolutionary anthropology and an antitheoretical narrative
history, and under the inspiration of Park and later
theorists they were to provide the basis for functionalist
sociology. In anthropology, Aristotelian influence had
resulted in the search for the origins of man, an under-
taking carried out to discover the purpose "for the sake of
which" man exists. Unable to penetrate the shrouds of
prehistory, anthropologists adopted the practice of com-
paring several culturally different societies and then arrang-
ing them in a temporal sequence. Assuming that progress is
inherent in change and that the direction of change is from
simple to complex forms, anthropologists arrayed their
collection of contemporary cultures to show a slow but
steady shift from "primitive" to "modern" structures.
Thus labeled, the cultures were then redefined as the stages
of development, and it was assumed that all of mankind
had actually passed through these stages. Actual historical
events were divided into two types—those that described
the stages of growth and those that did not. The former
were elevated to a legitimate place in the scientific study
of social process; the latter were relegated to the dustbin
of accidental events that served only to interfere with
natural developments. This radical separation has thus
prevented a truly systematic study of events. In its place
there has been constructed an evolutionist and cyclical
social science.

Despite the general acceptance of Aristotelian and evolutionist thinking in social science, Park's particular version
of it, the race-relations cycle, did not attract universal
acceptance. Problems of evidence showing the cycle's
operation, variations in the actual histories of races that

apparently contradict the theory, and the failure of blacks to reach the promised terminal stage of complete assimilation contribute to doubts about its theoretical value. However, rejection of the race-relations cycle has often been accompanied by a rejection of the possibility of any sociological theory in the field of race relations. Many sociologists have turned their attention to racial issues that appear more manageable: to the solution of particular social problems, the study of the psychology of race prejudice, and the development of programs to ameliorate the condition of racial minorities in America.

During the four decades that separate the formulation of Park's race-relations cycle and Parsons' citizenship or inclusion cycle, the sociology of race relations has been characterized primarily by studies of the psychology of race prejudice. Dollard provided a unique synthesis of community analysis and psychoanalytic thought in his delineation of the reciprocal "gains" to be made by blacks and whites within the South's caste order. Myrdal argued that the American Creed, which prevails in the hearts and minds of Americans, would eventually cause them to banish racism from their society; an ambiguous and contradictory psyche, Myrdal suggested, could not long endure its own unsteady state.

However, Allport and Adorno and his associates stressed the relative imperviousness of certain fixed mental states to change and were generally pessimistic in their analysis of the "curative" effects of programs designed to reduce prejudice, resolve tensions, and restore racial harmony. Parsons provided one of the most thoroughgoing analyses of the cultural basis for aggression in general and racial hostility in particular when he argued that Western values and institutions cannot help but engender deep-seated frustrations. These frustrations are first repressed, then displaced, and finally manifested in aggressive actions toward scapegoat groups.

Parsons' social psychology is far more pessimistic than Allport's. Allport conceives of racial prejudice as an outcome of maladaptations in the socialization process. Parsons sees it as an inevitable outcome of the strains imposed by Western civilization; aggression will be prevented only if present values are adjusted or exchanged for ones that do not engender frustrations. Parsons neither predicts nor proposes a cultural revolution, however. Consistent with Myrdal's conception of a dynamic social system striving to realize the unambiguous ideals of the American Creed, Parsons argues that the cyclical development of full citizenship for the black will remove the stigma of color and, presumably, lift from him the burden of prejudice. However, the causes of prejudice—unresolved frustrations—will persist, endemic to the system.

If, however, one questions Myrdal's assumption of the cultural and psychological priority of the American Creed, or if one subscribes to Dollard's reciprocity theory of black and white frustrations, aggressions, and relative gains, or finally, if one accepts Parsons' earlier statement that implies that blacks and Jews are likely to remain scapegoats in Western society, then one is hard pressed to be optimistic about the future of the black American.

Despite the contradictory arguments of these studies, they have supplied valuable insights on the race issue, sensitized many readers to hitherto unnoticed features of American life, and, with widely varying degrees of optimism, suggested that a resolution to the black problem might be found. However, in light of the original interest of racial sociology—to determine the origins, nature, structure, and future of black life in America—these studies are little more than deflective efforts. Concentration on the psychological aspects of the race issue tends to eschew the historical aspects of the question. Race cycles, for all their obvious faults, are attempts to deal, in a peculiar fashion to be sure, with the stubborn recalcitrance of the historical record. Only in a return to questions of history can sociologists reestablish their discipline's promise of a contribution to the study of race relations.

Parsons does provide such a return in his inclusion cycle, but it proves to be no advance over the theoretical stance of Park. Again there is a cycle composed of stages that are said to be inevitable—unless something interferes. Again there is a "comparative history," which illustrates the stages for *some* peoples, and from which Parsons deduces that the cycle is a valid historical sequence for *all* races in America. Again there is the introduction of a body of "obstacles" which may interfere with fulfillment of the cycle. And again the events of black history are divided into two categories, either confirming or contradicting the cycle, with the latter category relegated to "accidental" status. Although Parsons' conception of pluralism has disposed of the moral and ideological problem which made Park's so troublesome to social scientists, his adherence to discreditable Aristotelian and evolutionist ideas renders his cycle of little theoretical use to students of a science of history.

Parsons' approach pays little credence to the facts of black history or the values that blacks share. Except for his fears about the negative effects of black nationalism on the inclusion process, Parsons' approach, like that of all the other sociologists we have examined, eschews an examination of the actual nature of black life and black perspectives. If we are to understand the nature of black life, it is precisely these matters that deserve our most careful attention.

The Acceptance of History: An Anti-Aristotelian View

There has been a subterranean but powerful stream of anti-Aristotelian criticism in American sociology. The works of Frederick Teggart, Margaret T. Hodgen, Kenneth

E. Bock and, most recently, Robert A. Nisbet constitute a thorough critique of Aristotelian thought in American sociology and offer in lieu of it an approach to the scientific study of history that avoids the errors of the former school. Unfortunately, no sociologist has thought to apply this approach to the study of the black. Teggart, Hodgen, Bock, and Nisbet reject the original biological analogy that inspired Aristotle's perspective in favor of a quite different analytical conception of social science that, in Teggart's words, "must be founded upon a comparison of the particular histories of all human groups, and must be actuated by the conscious effort to take cognizance of all the available facts."[1] Theories of change must not assume that change is natural, nor should they assume the speed, mode, and direction of social motion *a priori*. Rather, investigators should, in the spirit and method of inquiry that inspired Hodgen's study of technological changes in England over the last eight centuries,[2] formulate specific hypotheses about the causes of change and subject them to the empirical validation available in the historical record. Further, as Bock has suggested, social science must regard "as a first step toward the formulation of testable statements of social or cultural processes, abandonment of the assumption that historical events are unique and acceptance of the assumption that there are discernible regularities in *all* historical occurrences."[3] Moreover, Bock continues, a true social science must unequivocally commit itself to a comparative study of actual events as they occurred in time and space and reject altogether the biological model that has up to now been employed as an analogue:

> Use of the biological analogy in any form and to any extent is unwarranted and dangerous. Considerations of the possible utility of analogical reasoning for conceptualization notwithstanding, the repeated experi-

ence of Western scholars over more than twenty-five hundred years demonstrates unequivocally that the analogy between society and an organism has worked uniformly to stop inquiry and to produce images of social process plainly contradicted by evidence at hand. The belief derived from analogy that society is a process of slow and continuous change generated and directed by potential present within the thing changing from the beginning, has served only to divert attention from the evidence that must be admitted in any candid search for processes—evidence that cannot be dismissed as "secondary" factors of "unnatural" interventions or "anti-evolutionary" forces.[4]

Finally, again quoting from Bock's penetrating critique, "Abandonment of the broader organic theory of change also carries with it a rejection of its subsidiary concepts. These include the notions that change has been always from the simple to the complex, from the homogeneous to the heterogeneous, or from the undifferentiated to the differentiated."[5]

What general concepts of change are relevant to a nonevolutionistic sociology?

Nisbet[6] has presented a discussion of these from which an inventory can be adduced. They are fixity or persistence; crisis and catastrophe; discontinuity and nonuniformity; and open-endedness or nondirectional change.

By citing fixity as a condition of nonevolutionistic development Nisbet is saying that stability, not change, is the required point of departure in any study of change. Most studies of change have started with the opposite assumption—*i.e.,* that change is both natural and continuous—so that they begged the very question under discussion. Applied to the study of the black, this concept of fixity reminds us that nothing is so common to the human condition as conservatism of habit and persistence of institutions. Rather than concentrating on cycles of assimilation, inclusion, or emergence—*i.e.,* projected trends which derive from an assumption about the naturalness and permanence of change—sociologists might first turn their attention to the persistent features of the black condition and then to the irregular and occasionally tumultuous challenges to these persistences. Such studies would concentrate on blacks in their everyday *being* and avoid the evolutionistic predictions about their *becoming.* They would focus on the structures of institutions, the sources of permanence, and the resistance to change. They would cite and date changes and search for the antecedent causes of those changes.

Crisis and catastrophe are among the crucial elements to be considered in developing a general theory of the sources of social change. W. I. Thomas first noted the relation of crisis to attention and thence to social change sixty years ago (strikingly consonant, incidentally, with today's most avant-garde and nonevolutionist sociology, the school known as ethnomethodology).[7]

If control over nature and other men is man's goal, Thomas observed, then attention "is the mental attitude which takes note of the outside world and manipulates it."[8] Whether attention is operant at any given time is a function of habit or crisis. In the former case, when matters are running smoothly, when people are behaving in a traditional and routine manner untroubled by emergencies, strains, or confusion, then attention is relaxed and conscious manipulation of the world is low. But when a crisis ensues—whether a natural disaster, a war, a sudden population change, an intrusion of a remarkable idea—then attention is maximized, consciousness comes to the fore, and innovative and modifying behavior is likely to begin. Some crises may be so severe as to destroy those experiencing them, but crises need not be violent. A crisis can be any event that causes a disturbance of habit, a shocking of the consciousness out of its habitual lethargy, a puzzlement over meanings, and some action taken to re-create stability.

Max Weber's famous study of the rise of capitalism is a good example of the kind of sociology being espoused here. Not only is it a brilliant refutation of the Marxist-evolutionist thesis that capitalism matured in the womb of the older society, but it is also a dramatic example of the crisis produced by a new idea and the changes that followed the full comprehension of that idea. As Nisbet points out, "What is of importance is the method: a genuinely historical method, one which proceeds from social behavior, from events, from concrete circumstances, rather than from . . . abstract categories."[9]

Weber produced no "natural history," relied on no evolutionary features; nor did he perceive capitalism as the inevitable outcome of historical forces. Rather, Weber showed how the introduction of Calvinism shattered the basic belief system of the West and was thus a decisive moment in history. The discovery that all was predestined, that God's will was impenetrable, and that man could do nothing to alter the foreordained future that God had designed led to a major crisis of conscience.[10] One resolution of this crisis was that plunge into uncertainty taken by the Puritans, who in the face of God's awful void undertook the most risky of actions in order to discover signs of their salvation or damnation. In the process they created capitalism.

Might not the history of the black be studied with this same methodology? Utilizing the Weberian model, we might note that the Africans' encounter with European slave traders must have produced a crisis among the Africans equal to that caused by Calvinism among the Europeans. Indeed there is ample evidence that just such a crisis occurred: Kidnapped Africans wrote about the shocking, puzzling, and indeed inexplicable events that befell them while on the march to the Guinea coast, aboard the slave ships, and in the towns and plantations of the New World.[11]

How did blacks resolve this crisis—their realization that once having been sold or kidnapped and herded aboard a slave ship, nothing would ever be the same again for them? Little if any work has been done to answer this question, although precisely the kind of materials which Weber used—*i.e.,* biographies and accounts, in the form of slave narratives—are available.

Still other cases for Weberian analysis are found in the post-Emancipation period. Again blacks were thrust into a new and puzzling world, that of the nominally free man. Surrounded by hostile whites, attacked by the night riders of the Ku Klux Klan, and possessed of few educational and material resources, blacks were thrown back upon their own capacities to cope with crisis. On several occasions when integration appeared a likely possibility, black leaders have espoused back-to-Africa movements,[12] cultural nationalism,[13] or resistance to the blandishments of the American promise.[14] Such movements introduced a dissonance into everyday life, created doubts and anxieties as well as challenges among blacks, and in general produced the kind of crisis which required agonizing reappraisal of individual and group identity.[15]

In general, it may be concluded that throughout his history the black man in America has been confronted suddenly and irregularly by new possibilities which tested his individual and collective mettle.[16] The response to these crises, the development of innovative ways of life, the challenges flung at an unknown destiny, the all-too-rare triumphs, and the frequent tragedies are the stuff of a grand sociology that has yet to be written.

In contrast to the regular, orderly, and continuous progress embodied in the cycle theories, actual life would suggest the relevance of discontinuity, of persistence punctuated by eruption, of irregularities and lack of uniformity. W. I. Thomas pointed out that the response to a crisis would not be uniform among peoples since it would depend on the presence of charismatic leaders among them, the level of culture at which they live, and "the character of the ideas by which the group-mind is prepossessed."[17]

In analyzing the black in America, it would seem to follow, sociologists would do well to keep in mind the irregularities of situations, the chance and spontaneous elements in response, and the various intellectual, moral, and material resources which can be brought to bear. In addition, the obdurate and recalcitrant nature of the world against which blacks move is of crucial importance. Rather than a unilinear march along a single track, black life in America might be likened to water poured on porous cement: Although the material appears impregnable, the different drops and streams find their own way through the interstices which are not apparent to the casual observer. Sometimes movement is halted altogether; sometimes a circuitous route has to be discovered; and sometimes the water must build up enough pressure to push through a hard surface. Nothing, then, is orderly, progressive, and continuous as in a foreordained cycle. Instead, it is always a case of man in conflict—with nature, with fellow men, and with himself. And the final outcome is unknown.

Finally, and in application of Nisbet's fourth basic concept, nothing would seem more true about the black in America than the fact that his present is problematic, his past unknown, and his future uncertain. For a sociology of blacks to remain faithful to its purpose, it would have to acknowledge this condition—a condition which is properly called *absurd*.[18] From his abrupt and involuntary exile from Africa, through the horrors of the sea passage, the cruelties and debilitation of slavery, and the ironies of unfreedom in a nominally free condition, down to the ambiguous promises of equality and the exotic seductions of negritude and Africa, the black man has been resident in a less than reasonable world, a world not only denied the illumination of the past but also frequently shorn of hope for the future. Camus describes such a world thus:

> In a universe that is suddenly deprived of illusions and of light, man feels a stranger. His is an irremediable exile, because he is deprived of memories of a lost homeland as much as he lacks the hope of a promised land to come. This divorce between man and his life, the actor and his setting, truly constitutes the feeling of absurdity.[19]

The black has been deprived of his history, and with this deprivation not only the past but also the future is wiped out: He has neither known predecessors to provide tradition nor unambiguously defined successors to instill promise.[20] "To visit a people who have no history," Archibald D. Murphey once wrote, "is like going into a wilderness where there are no roads to direct a traveller. The people have nothing to which they can look back; the wisdom and acts of their forefathers are forgotten; the experience of one generation is lost to the succeeding one; and the consequence is, that people have little attachment to their state."[21]

The world of such people is persistently puzzling. To this puzzle of existence they must bring to bear whatever resources they possess, whatever imagination and intelligence they can provide, whatever genius resides among them. Such is the conscious world of the Negro; to such ought to be dedicated the sociology of the black man.

Notes

CHAPTER 1

Social Darwinism
and the Sociological Study of the Black American

1. See L. L. Bernard, "Henry Hughes, First American Sociologist," *Social Forces*, XV (December, 1936), pp. 154-74, and "The Historic Pattern of Sociology in the South." *Social Forces*, XVI (October, 1937), pp. 1-12.

2. For discussions of the contributions of these men to sociology, see L. L. Bernard and Jessie Bernard, *Origins of American Sociology: The Social Science Movement in the United States* (New York, Russell and Russell, 1965), pp. 500 10, 838 40; Harry Elmer Barnes, "William Graham Sumner: Spencerianism in American Dress" and "Lester Frank Ward: The Reconstruction of Society by Social Science," in Harry Elmer Barnes, ed., *An Introduction to the History of Sociology* (Chicago, University of Chicago Press, 1948), pp. 155-72, 173-90; and Charles H. Page, *Class and American Sociology: From Ward to Ross* (New York, Schocken Books, 1969), pp. 29-112.

3. See Harry Elmer Barnes, "William Isaac Thomas: The Fusion of Psychological and Cultural Sociology," in Barnes. *op.cit.*, pp. 793-804; Alvin Boskoff, *Theory in American Sociology: Major Sources and Applications* (New York, Thomas Y. Crowell, 1969), pp. 61-80; Morris Janowitz, "Introduction," in *W. I.*

Thomas on Social Organization and Personality (Chicago, University of Chicago Press, Phoenix Books, 1966), pp. *vii-lviii;* Edmund H. Volkhart, ed., *Social Behavior and Personality: Contributions of W. I. Thomas to Theory and Social Research* (New York, Social Science Research Council, 1951); Herbert Blumer, *An Appraisal of Thomas and Znaniecki's the Polish Peasant in Europe and America* (New York, Social Science Research Council, 1946); and Donald W. Ball, "The Definition of the Situation: Some Theoretical and Methodological Consequences of Taking W. I. Thomas Seriously," in Jack D. Douglas, ed., *Existential Sociology* (New York, Appleton-Century-Crofts, forthcoming).

4. See Richard Dewey, "Charles Horton Cooley: Pioneer in Psychosociology," in Barnes, *op.cit.,* pp. 833-52; and Albert J. Reiss, Jr., ed., *Cooley and Sociological Analysis* (Ann Arbor, University of Michigan Press, 1968).

5. See Stanford M. Lyman, "The Race Relations Cycle of Robert E. Park," *Pacific Sociological Review,* II (Spring, 1968), pp. 16-22; Seymour Martin Lipset, "Changing Social Status and Prejudice: The Race Theories of a Pioneering American Sociologist," *Commentary,* 9 (May, 1950), pp. 475-79; Robert E. Lee Faris, Jr., *Chicago Sociology, 1920-1932* (San Francisco, Chandler Publishing Company, 1967), pp. 20-134; and Boskoff, *op. cit.,* pp. 94-111.

6. For a review of Myrdal's work see John Madge, *The Origins of Scientific Sociology* (New York, Free Press, 1962), pp. 255-86.

7. T. W. Adorno, Else Frenkel-Brunswick, Daniel J. Levinson, R. Nevitt Stanford, *et al., The Authoritarian Personality* (New York, Harper and Row, 1950).

8. William Stanton, *The Leopard's Spots: Scientific Attitudes Toward Race in America, 1815-1859* (Chicago, University of Chicago Press, 1966).

9. Fitzhugh's two major works, *Sociology for the South* and *Cannibals All!*, are reprinted in Harvey Wish, ed., *Ante-Bellum: Writings of George Fitzhugh and Hinton Rowan Helper on Slavery* (New York, Capricorn Books, 1960).

10. The final two chapters of Hughes' *Treatise* are reprinted in Eric L. McKitrick, ed., *Slavery Defended: The Views of the Old South* (Englewood Cliffs, N. J., Prentice-Hall, 1963), pp. 51-56.

11. See Richard Hofstadter, *Social Darwinism in American Thought* (Boston, Beacon Press, 1955); and Robert E. Lee Faris, "Evolution and American Sociology," in Stow Persons, ed., *Evolutionary Thought in America* (New York, George Braziller, 1956), pp. 160-81.

12. William Graham Sumner, *Folkways: A Study of the Sociological Importance of Usages, Manners, Customs, Mores, and Morals* (Boston, Ginn and Co., 1940).

13. William Graham Sumner, "The Absurd Effort to Make the World Over," in Stow Persons, ed., *Social Darwinism: Selected Essays of William Graham Sumner* (Englewood Cliffs, N.J., Prentice-Hall, 1963), pp. 163-80.

14. Sumner, *Folkways, op. cit.*, p. 77. For a vigorous dissent see E. Franklin Frazier, "Theoretical Structure of Sociology and Social Research," in G. Franklin Edwards, ed., *E. Franklin Frazier on Race Relations* (Chicago, University of Chicago Press, 1968), p. 5.

15. Sumner, *Folkways, op. cit.*, pp. 77-78.

16. Lester Frank Ward, *Outline of Sociology* (New York, Macmillan, 1913), pp. 180-90.

17. Ludwig Gumplowicz, *Outlines of Sociology*, Irving Louis Horowitz, ed. (New York, Paine-Whitman, 1963), pp. 199-237; see also Harry Elmer Barnes, "The Social Philosophy of Ludwig Gumplowicz: The Struggles of Races and Social Groups," in Barnes, *op. cit.*, pp. 191-208.

18. See Robert Schmid, "Gustav Ratzenhofer: Sociological Positivism and the Theory of Social Interests," in Barnes, *op. cit.*, pp. 374-84.

19. Lester Frank Ward, "Evolution of Social Structure," *American Journal of Sociology*, X (March, 1905), pp. 589-605; reprinted in Henry Steele Commager, ed., *Lester Ward and the Welfare State* (Indianapolis, Ind., Bobbs-Merrill, 1967), p. 334.

20. Lester F. Ward, *Applied Sociology: A Treatise on the Conscious Improvement of Society by Society* (Boston, Ginn and Co., 1905), p. 110.

21. Lester F. Ward, "Evolution of Social Structure," in Commager, *op. cit.*, p. 340.

22. Lester F. Ward, "Dynamic Sociology," in Commager, *op. cit.*, p. 54.

23. William I. Thomas, "The Psychology of Race Prejudice," *American Journal of Sociology*, IX (March, 1904), p. 609.

24. *Ibid.*, pp. 609-10.

25. See the suggestion that interracial cooperatives would promote racial harmony in W. I. Thomas and Florian Znaniecki, *The Polish Peasant in Europe and America,* Vol. II (New York, Dover Publications, 1958), p. 1826.

26. Charles Horton Cooley, *Social Organization: A Study of the Larger Mind,* in *The Two Major Works of Charles Horton Cooley: Human Nature and the Social Order and Social Organization* (Glencoe, Ill., Free Press, 1956), p. 218.

27. Charles Horton Cooley, *Social Process* (Carbondale, Southern Illinois University Press, 1966), p. 274.

28. *Ibid.*, p. 280

29. Charles Horton Cooley, *Social Organizations, op. cit.*, p. 220.

30. Robert E. Park, *Race and Culture*, Vol. I, *Collected Papers of Robert E. Park*, Everett C. Hughes *et al.*, eds. (Glencoe, Ill., Free Press, 1950), pp. 150-51.

31. Louis Wirth, "The Problem of Minority Groups," in Ralph Linton, ed., *The Science of Man in the World Crisis* (New York, Columbia University Press, 1945), pp. 347-72.

32. John Dollard, *Caste and Class in a Southern Town*, 3d ed. (Garden City, N.Y., Doubleday, 1957); Hortense Powdermaker, *After Freedom: A Cultural Study in the Deep South* (New York, Atheneum, 1968); Allison Davis, Burleigh B. Gardner, and Mary R. Gardner, *Deep South: A Social Anthropological Study of Caste and Class*, abr. ed., (Chicago, University of Chicago Press, 1965); Allison Davis and John Dollard, *Children of Bondage: The Personality Development of Negro Youth in the Urban South* (New York, Harper and Row, 1964); and Hylan Lewis, *Blackways of Kent* (Chapel Hill, University of North Carolina Press, 1955).

33. Gunnar Myrdal *et al., An American Dilemma* (New York, Harper and Bros., 1944).

34. Gordon W. Allport, "Prejudice: A Study in Psychological and Social Causation," in Talcott Parsons and Edward A. Shils, eds., *Toward a General Theory of Action: Theoretical Foun-*

dations for the Social Sciences (New York, Harper and Row, 1962), pp. 365-87; and *The Nature of Prejudice* (Garden City, N.Y., Doubleday Anchor, 1958).

35. For a summary of these studies see George Eaton Simpson and J. Milton Yinger, *Racial and Cultural Minorities: An Analysis of Prejudice and Discrimination,* 3d ed. (New York, Harper and Row, 1965), pp. 491-521.

36. T. W. Adorno *et al., op. cit.*

37. See Frank R. Westie, "Race and Ethnic Relations," in Robert E. Lee Faris, Jr., *Handbook of Modern Sociology* (Chicago, Rand, McNally, 1964), p. 576; George E. Simpson and J. Milton Yinger, "The Sociology of Race and Ethnic Relations," in Robert K. Merton, Leonard Broom, Leonard S. Cottrell, Jr., *Sociology Today: Problems and Prospects* (New York, Basic Books, 1959), p. 376; and Everett C. Hughes, "Race Relations and The Sociological Imagination," *American Sociological Review*, 28 (December, 1963), pp. 879-90.

38. Richard McKeon, ed., *The Basic Works of Aristotle* (New York, Random House, 1941), pp. 218-52, 1127-76.

39. See Kenneth E. Bock, "Darwin and Social Theory," *Philosophy of Science*, 22 (April, 1955), pp. 123-34; "Evolution, Function, and Change," *American Sociological Review*, 28 (April, 1936), pp. 229-37; and "Theories of Progress and Evolution," in Werner J. Cahnman and Alvin Boskoff, eds., *Sociology and History: Theory and Research* (New York, Free Press of Glencoe, 1964), pp. 21-44.

40. See Marvin B. Scott, "Functional Foibles and the Analysis of Social Change," *Inquiry*, 9 (1966), pp. 205-14.

41. Frederick Teggart, *The Theory and Processes of History* (Berkeley, University of California Press, 1941).

42. Margaret T. Hodgen, *Change and History: A Study of the Dated Distributions of Technological Innovations in England* (Viking Fund Publications in Anthropology, No. 18; New York, Wenner-Gren Fund for Anthropological Research, 1952); and *Early Anthropology in the Sixteenth and Seventeenth Century* (Philadelphia, University of Pennsylvania Press, 1964).

43. Kenneth E. Bock, *The Acceptance of Histories: Toward a Perspective for Social Science* (University of California

Publications in Sociology and Social Institutions, Vol. III, No. 1; Berkeley, University of California Press,. 1956).

44. Robert A. Nisbet, *Social Change and History* (New York, Oxford University Press, 1969).

CHAPTER II

The Race-Relations Cycle of Robert E. Park

1. Robert E. Park, "Our Racial Frontier on the Pacific," *Race and Culture*, Vol. I, *The Collected Papers of Robert Ezra Park*, Everett C. Hughes *et al.*, eds. (Glencoe, Ill., Free Press, 1950), p. 150.

2. The following is adapted from Kenneth E. Bock, *The Acceptance of Histories: Toward a Perspective for Social Science* (University of California Publications in Sociology and Social Institutions, Vol. III, No. 1; Berkeley, University of California Press, 1956), pp. 49-53.

3. Aristotle, *Metaphysics,* trans. by W. D. Ross, Bk. XI, Chap. 8, in *Basic Works of Aristotle*, Richard McKeon, ed. (New York, Random House, 1941), p. 862.

4. Aristotle, *Politics*, trans. by Benjamin Jowett, Bk. 1, Chap. 2, in *Basic Works of Aristotle, op. cit.*, pp. 1127-29.

5. *Ibid.*, p. 1129; Bock, *op. cit.*, p. 51.

6. Winifred Raushenbush, "Their Place in the Sun," *Survey Graphic*, LVI (May, 1926), pp. 141-45.

7. Raushenbush, "The Great Wall of Chinatown," *Survey Graphic*, LVI (May, 1926), pp. 154-59.

8. Elliot Grinnel Mears, "The Land, the Crops, and the Oriental," *Survey Graphic*, LVI (May, 1926), pp. 146-50; R. D. McKenzie, "The Oriental Finds a Job," *ibid.*, pp. 151-53; Kazuo Kawai, "Three Roads, and None Easy," *ibid.*, pp. 164-66; and William C. Smith, "Born American, But–," *ibid.*, pp. 167-68.

9. Raushenbush, "Their Place in the Sun," *op. cit.*, p. 144.

10. *Ibid.*, p. 144.

11. Park, "Behind Our Masks," *Race and Culture, op. cit.*, p. 254.

12. Park, "The Race Relations Cycle in Hawaii," *Race and Culture, op. cit.*, pp. 189-95.
13. Park, "An Autobiographical Note," *Race and Culture, op. cit.*, pp. *vii-viii*.
14. "Looking at race relations in the long historical perspective, this modern world which seems destined to bring presently all the diverse and distant peoples of the earth together within the limits of a common culture and a common social order, strikes one as something not merely unique but millennial. Nevertheless, this new civilization is the product of essentially the same historical processes as those that preceded it. The same forces which brought about the diversity of races will inevitably bring about, in the long run, a diversity in the peoples of the modern world corresponding to that which we have seen in the old. It is likely, however, that these diversities will be based in the future less on inheritance and race and rather more on culture and occupation. That means that race conflicts in the modern world, which is already or presently will be a single great society, will be more and more in the future confused with, and eventually superseded by, the conflicts of classes." Robert E. Park, "The Nature of Race Relations," in *Race Relations and the Race Problem: A Symposium on a Growing National and International Problem with Special Reference to the South*, Edgar T. Thompson, ed. (Durham, N.C., Duke University Press, 1939), p. 45.
15. Park, "Racial Assimilation in Secondary Groups with Special Reference to the Negro," *Race and Culture, op. cit.*, p. 207.
16. *Ibid.*, p. 209.
17. Park, "The Negro and His Plantation Heritage," *Race and Culture, op. cit.*, p. 76.
18. Park, "Racial Assimilation in Secondary Groups," *Race and Culture, op. cit.*, p. 209.
19. Park, "Education in Relation to the Conflict and Fusion of Cultures: With Special Reference to the Problems of the Immigrant, the Negro, and Missions," *Race and Culture, op. cit.*, p. 267. The terms of this debate seem to have been set by Melville Herskovitz on one side and Park's disciple E. Franklin Frazier on the other. See Herskovitz, *The Myth of the Negro Past* (Boston, Beacon Press, 1958); *The New World Negro:*

Selected Papers in Afroamerican Studies, Frances S. Herskovitz, ed. (Bloomington, Indiana University Press, 1966); Frazier, *The Negro Family in the United States*, rev. ed. (Chicago, University of Chicago Press, 1966), pp. 3-69; and *The Negro in the United States*, rev. ed. (New York, Macmillan, 1957), pp. 3-21.

20. Compare, for example, Ulrich Bonnell Phillips, *American Negro Slavery: A Survey of the Supply, Employment and Control of Negro Labor as Determined by the Plantation Regime* (Gloucester, Mass., Peter Smith, 1959) with Kenneth M. Stampp, *The Peculiar Institution: Slavery in the Ante-Bellum South* (New York, Alfred A. Knopf, 1963) and with Stanley Elkins, *Slavery: A Problem in American Institutional and Intellectual Life* (Chicago, University of Chicago Press, 1959).

21. Park, "The Bases of Race Prejudice," *Race and Culture, op. cit.*, p. 234.

22. Park, "Racial Assimilation in Secondary Groups," *Race and Culture, op. cit.*, pp. 209-10.

23. William James, *Talks to Teachers on Psychology and to Students on Some of Life's Ideals* (New York, Henry Holt, 1914).

24. Park, *Race and Culture, op. cit.*, pp. 50, 66-70, 329-30.

25. Park, "Behind Our Masks," *Race and Culture, op. cit.*, pp. 244-55.

26. Park, "Personality and Cultural Conflict," *Race and Culture, op. cit.*, pp. 360-63.

27. Park, "Racial Assimilation in Secondary Groups," *Race and Culture, op. cit.*, pp. 208-9.

28. Park, "Education in Its Relation to Cultures." *Race and Culture, op. cit.*, p. 280.

29. *Ibid.*

30. *Ibid.*, p. 281.

31. *Ibid.*, p. 269.

32. *Ibid.*, p. 279.

33. *Ibid.*, p. 281.

34. *Ibid.*, p. 280.

35. *Ibid.* This statement, perhaps more than any other, earned Park the enmity of blacks. The most scathing indictment is that of writer Ralph Ellison. Reminding his readers that Park was Booker T. Washington's secretary, or in Ellison's own

words "the man responsible for inflating Tuskegee into a national symbol" and the man "who is sometimes spoken of as the 'power behind Washington's throne,'" Ellison compared him to William Graham Sumner in terms of his assumptions. After quoting the statement on temperament, he concludes: "Park's descriptive metaphor is so pregnant with mixed motives as to birth a thousand compromises and indecisions. Imagine the effect such teachings had upon Negro students alone! Thus what started as part of a democratic attitude, ends not only uncomfortably close to the preachings of Sumner, but to those of Dr. Goebbels as well."—Ralph Ellison, *"An American Dilemma*: A Review," in *Shadow and Act* (New York, Random House, 1964). p. 308.

In defense of Park's usage of the "lady among the races" phrase Morris Janowitz has written: "Park regretted it again and again. But that is of little consequence. What is central is that Park, following on W. I. Thomas, was destroying biological racism and was searching for a new vocabulary of intergroup relations. And it is equally unfair to hold sociologists responsible for the misuse of their concepts by those seeking to maintain the status quo." Morris Janowitz, "Review of *Shadow and Act," American Journal of Sociology*, LXX (May, 1965), p. 733.

36. Park, "Education in Its Relation to Cultures," *Race and Culture, op. cit.*, p. 281.
37. *Ibid.*
38. Park, "The Concept of Social Distance As Applied to the Study of Racial Attitudes and Racial Relations," *Race and Culture, op. cit.*, p. 259.
39. Park, "Race Prejudice and Japanese American Relations," *Race and Culture, op. cit.*, p. 277.
40. *Ibid.*, pp. 228-29.
41. Park, "The Bases of Race Prejudice," *Race and Culture, op. cit.*, pp. 230-31.
42. *Ibid.*, p. 233.
43. *Ibid.*, p. 234.
44. Park, "Our Racial Frontier on the Pacific," *Race and Culture, op. cit.*, p. 150.
45. *Ibid.*

46. *Ibid.*, pp. 150-51.
47. Park, "Racial Relations in Secondary Groups," *Race and Culture, op. cit.*, pp. 211-20.
48. Park, "The Bases of Race Prejudice," *Race and Culture, op. cit.*, pp. 238-39.
49. *Ibid.*
50. Park, "Racial Assimilation in Secondary Groups with Particular Reference to the Negro," *Race and Culture, op. cit.*, p. 209.
51. Park, "The Bases of Race Prejudice," *Race and Culture, op. cit.*, pp. 238-39.
52. *Ibid.*, p. 239.
53. *Ibid.*, pp. 239-41.
54. Park, "Our Racial Frontier on the Pacific," *Race and Culture, op. cit.*, p. 151.
55. Seymour Martin Lipset, "Changing Social Status and Prejudice: The Race Theories of a Pioneering American Sociologist," *Commentary*, 9 (May, 1950), p. 479.
56. Louis Wirth, *The Ghetto* (Chicago, University of Chicago Press, Phoenix Books, 1956).
57. Rose Hum Lee, *The Chinese in the United States of America* (Hong Kong, Hong Kong University Press, 1960). For further discussion of this work see Stanford M. Lyman, "Overseas Chinese in America and Indonesia," *Pacific Affairs*, XXXIV (Winter, 1961-62), pp. 380-89.
58. Louis Wirth, "The Problem of Minority Groups," in *The Science of Man in the World Crisis*, Ralph Linton, ed. (New York, Columbia University Press, 1945), p. 364.
59. W. Lloyd Warner and Leo Srole, *The Social Systems of American Ethnic Groups* (Yankee City Series, Vol. III; New Haven, Conn., Yale University Press, 1945), pp. 283-96.
60. James W. Vander Zanden, *American Minority Relations* (New York, Ronald Press, 1963), p. 277.
61. See Stanford M. Lyman, "Contrasts in the Community Organization of Chinese and Japanese in North America," *Canadian Review of Sociology and Anthropology*, 2 (May, 1968), pp. 51-67.
62. Emory S. Bogardus, "A Race Relations Cycle," *American Journal of Sociology*, 35 (January, 1930), pp. 612-17; Robert

H. Ross and E. S. Bogardus, "The Second Generation Race Relations Cycle: A Study in Issei-Nisei Relationships," *Sociology and Social Research*, 24 (March, 1940), pp. 357-63. See also Bogardus, "Current Problems of Japanese Americans," *Sociology and Social Research*, 25 (September, 1940), pp. 63-66.

63. Jitsuichi Masuoka, "Race Relations and Nisei Problems," *Sociology and Social Research*, 30 (July, 1946), pp. 452-59.

64. W. O. Brown, "Culture Contact and Race Conflict," in E. B. Reuter, ed., *Race and Culture Contacts* (New York, McGraw-Hill, 1934), pp. 34-37.

65. Clarence E. Glick, "Social Roles and Types in Race Relations," in A. W. Lind, ed., *Race Relations in World Perspective* (Honolulu, University of Hawaii Press, 1955), pp. 239-41; Stanley Lieberson, "A Societal Theory of Race and Ethnic Relations," *American Sociological Review*, 26 (December, 1961), pp. 902-10.

66. Amitai Etzioni, "The Ghetto—A Re-Evaluation," *Social Forces*, 37 (March, 1959), pp. 255-62.

67. Brewton Berry, *Race and Ethnic Relations*, 3d ed. (Boston, Houghton Mifflin, 1965), p. 135. In his later work on certain groups of racial hybrids in America, *Almost White* (New York, Macmillan, 1963), Berry avoids theoretical issues and, instead, concentrates on pleading for understanding and compassion. See Stanford M. Lyman, "The Spectrum of Color," *Social Research*, 31 (Autumn, 1964), pp. 364-73.

68. Tamotsu Shibutani and Kian Moon Kwan, *Ethnic Stratification: A Comparative Approach* (New York, Macmillan, 1965), pp. 116-35.

69. Ernest W. Burgess, "The Growth of the City: An Introduction to a Research Project," in Robert E. Park, Ernest W. Burgess, and Roderick D. McKenzie, eds., *The City* (Chicago, University of Chicago Press, 1967), pp. 47-62.

70. E. Franklin Frazier, "The Impact of Urban Civilization upon Negro Family Life," *American Sociological Review*, II (August, 1937), pp. 609-18. Reprinted in Norman W. Bell and Ezra F. Vogel, eds., *A Modern Introduction to the Family* (Toronto, Macmillan of Canada, 1960), pp. 101-11.

71. *Ibid.*, p. 109.

72. *Ibid*.
73. Frazier, *The Negro Family in the United States*, rev. and abr. ed. (Chicago, University of Chicago Press, 1966), pp. 237-38.
74. Frazier, *The Negro Family in Chicago* (Chicago, University of Chicago Press, 1932), p. 103.
75. Frazier, "Negro Harlem: An Ecological Study," *American Journal of Sociology*, 43 (July, 1937), p. 88.
76. Louis Wirth, "Types of Nationalism," *American Journal of Sociology*, XLI (May, 1936), pp. 723-37.
77. Wirth, "The Problem of Minority Groups," *op. cit*., pp. 354-64.
78. *Ibid*., p. 364.
79. Frazier, *The Negro in the United States*, rev. ed. (New York, Macmillan, 1957), p. 14.
80. *Ibid*., p. 21.
81. *Ibid*., pp. 123-46.
82. *Ibid*., pp. 147-70.
83. *Ibid*., pp. 171-416.
84. Frazier, *Negro Youth at the Crossways: Their Personality Development in the Middle States* (New York, Schocken Books, 1967).
85. Frazier, "The Negro's Vested Interest in Segregation," in *Race Prejudice and Discrimination: Readings in Intergroup Relations in the United States*, Arnold M. Rose, ed. (New York, Alfred A. Knopf, 1953), pp. 332-39.
86. Frazier, *The Negro Church in America* (New York, Schocken Books, 1963).
87. See Amy Jacques Garvey, comp., *The Philosophy and Opinions of Marcus Garvey*, 2d ed. (London, Frank Cass, 1967); and Edmund David Cronon, *Black Moses: The Story of Marcus Garvey and the Universal Negro Improvement Association* (Madison, University of Wisconsin Press, 1964).
88. Frazier, *The Negro in the United States*, *op. cit*., pp. 680-81.
89. *Ibid*., pp. 567-664.
90. Emory S. Bogardus, "A Race Relations Cycle," *op. cit*.
91. Frazier, *The Negro in the United States*, *op. cit*., pp. 687-706.
92. See, *e.g.*, Park, *Race and Culture*, *op. cit*., p. 251.
93. Frazier, *Black Bourgeoisie: The Rise of a New Middle Class in the United States* (Glencoe, Ill., Free Press, 1957), p. 238.

94. Park, "Our Racial Frontier on the Pacific," *Race and Culture*, *op. cit.,* p. 151.

95. Frazier, *Race and Culture Contacts in the Modern World* (New York, Alfred A. Knopf, 1957).

96. *Ibid*., p. 338.

97. In 1953 Frazier lectured in England on the race relations cycle in the United States, noting: "In conformity with our conception of sociology, the general characteristics of the systems of social relationships which emerge during the course of race and culture contacts will be analyzed. The scheme presented here represents a logical rather than a chronological scheme for the study of the problem though it provides an evolutionary frame of reference for studying the character of race relations."—"The Theoretical Structure of Sociology and Sociological Research," *British Journal of Sociology*, 4 (December, 1953), reprinted in *E. Franklin Frazier on Race Relations*, G. Franklin Edwards, ed. (Chicago, University of Chicago Press, 1968), p. 9.

98. Frazier, "Racial Problems in World Society," in *Race Relations: Problems and Theory*, Jitsuichi Masuoka and Preston Valien, eds. (Chapel Hill, University of North Carolina Press, 1961), p. 40.

CHAPTER III

Southern Gothic: Caste and Race in Southern Society

1. Horace R. Cayton, "The American Negro—A World Problem," *Social Education,* VIII, 5 (May, 1944), p. 208. The statement is contained in a letter from Park to Cayton.

2. Robert Park to Horace Cayton. Quoted in Horace R. Cayton, "Robert Park: A Great Man Died but Leaves Keen Observation on Our Democracy," *Pittsburgh Courier*, February 26, 1944. I am indebted to Mr. Cayton for turning over to me a typed copy of his obituary to Park.

3. Robert E. Park and Ernest W. Burgess, *Introduction to the Science of Sociology* (Chicago, University of Chicago Press, 1921), p. 665.

4. *Ibid.*
5. *Ibid.*
6. See Thomas L. Hartshorne, *The Distorted Image: Changing Conceptions of the American Character Since Turner* (Cleveland, The Press of Case Western Reserve University, 1968), pp. 123-33. See also Marie Jahoda, "The Migration of Psychoanalysis: Its Impact on American Psychology," in *The Intellectual Migration: Europe and America, 1930-1960*, Donald Fleming and Bernard Bailyn, eds. (Cambridge, Belknap Press of Harvard University Press, 1969), pp. 420-45.
7. John Dollard, *Caste and Class in a Southern Town*, 3d ed. (Garden City, N.Y., Doubleday Anchor Books, 1957).
8. *Ibid.*, p. 31.
9. *Ibid.*, p. 60.
10. *Ibid.*, pp. 203-4.
11. *Ibid.*, pp. 223-24.
12. *Ibid.*, p. 207.
13. *Ibid.*, p. 212.
14. W. I. Thomas and Florian Znaniecki, *The Polish Peasant in Europe and America*, Vol. II (New York, Dover Publications, 1958), pp. 1117-23.
15. Dollard, *op. cit.*, p. 156.
16. *Ibid.*, p. 177.
17. *Ibid.*, p. 174.
18. *Ibid.*
19. *Ibid.*, p. 185.
20. *Ibid.*
21. *Ibid.*, p. 187.
22. *Ibid.*, p. 255.
23. *Ibid.*, p. 262.
24. *Ibid.*, p. 266.
25. *Ibid.*, p. 433.
26. *Ibid.*, p. 440.
27. *Ibid.*, p. x.
28. *Ibid.*, p. xii.
29. *Ibid.*, p. xi.
30. *Ibid.*

31. Charles S. Johnson, *Shadow of the Plantation* (Chicago, University of Chicago Press, Phoenix Books, 1966).
32. Allison Davis, Burleigh B. Gardner, and Mary R. Gardner, *Deep South: A Social Anthropological Study of Caste and Class*, abr. ed. (Chicago, University of Chicago Press, Phoenix Books, 1965).
33. Hortense Powdermaker, *After Freedom: A Cultural Study in the Deep South* (Studies in American Negro Life; New York, Atheneum, 1968).
34. Hylan Lewis, *Blackways of Kent* (Chapel Hill, University of North Carolina Press, 1955).
35. Gerald D. Berreman, "Caste in India and the United States," *American Journal of Sociology*, LXVI, 2 (September, 1960), pp. 120-27.
36. See Andrew D. Weinberger, "A Reappraisal of the Constitutionality of 'Miscegenation' Statutes. State Legislation Against Mixed Marriages in the United States," Appendix G, in Ashley Montagu, *Man's Most Dangerous Myth: The Fallacy of Race* (Cleveland, World Publishing Co., Meridian Books, 1965), pp. 402-24.
37. St. Clair Drake and Horace R. Cayton, *Black Metropolis: A Study of Negro Life in a Northern City*, Vol. I (New York, Harper Torchbooks, 1962), pp. 117-28.
38. Frank F. Lee, *Negro and White in a Connecticut Town* (New Haven, Conn., College and University Press, 1961).
39. Weinberger, *op. cit.*
40. Leon F. Litwack, *North of Slavery: The Negro in the Free States, 1790-1860* (Chicago, University of Chicago Press, Phoenix Books, 1965).
41. Eugene H. Berwanger, *The Frontier Against Slavery: Western Anti-Negro Prejudice and the Slavery Extension Controversy* (Urbana, University of Illinois Press, 1967).
42. Louis Ruchames, *Racial Thought in America: From the Puritans to Abraham Lincoln* (Amherst, University of Massachusetts Press, 1969).
43. I. A. Newby, *Jim Crow's Defense: Anti-Negro Thought in America, 1900-1930* (Baton Rouge, Louisiana State University Press, 1965).

44. Eugene Genovese, "Southern Exposure," *New York Review of Books*, XIII (September 11, 1969), pp. 27-30. For Genovese's works on the subject see his *Political Economy of Slavery: Studies in the Economy and Society of the Slave South* (New York, Pantheon Books, 1956) and *The World the Slaveholders Made: Two Essays in Interpretation* (New York, Pantheon Books, 1969). For some penetrating reconsiderations of black history see C. Vann Woodward, "White Racism and Black 'Emancipation,' " *New York Review of Books,* XII (February 27, 1969), pp. 5-11; and J. H. Plumb, "Slavery, Race and the Poor," *New York Review of Books,* XII (March 13, 1969), pp. 3-5.

45. Winthrop D. Jordan, *White Over Black: American Attitudes Toward the Negro, 1550-1812* (Chapel Hill, University of North Carolina Press, 1968).

46. Thomas F. Gossett, *Race: The History of an Idea in America* (Dallas, Southern Methodist University Press, 1963).

47. Lee Eldridge Huddleston, *Origins of the American Indians: European Concepts, 1492-1792* (Austin, University of Texas Press, 1967); and Alden T. Vaughan, *New England Frontier: Puritans and Indians, 1620-1675* (Boston, Little, Brown, 1965).

CHAPTER IV

Gunnar Myrdal's *An American Dilemma*

1. Gunnar Myrdal, with the assistance of Richard Sterner and Arnold Rose, *An American Dilemma: The Negro Problem and Modern Democracy* (New York, Harper and Brothers, 1944).

2. George Washington Williams, *The History of the Negro in the United States* (New York, Bergman Publishers, 1968).

3. The following draws upon Appendix 2, "A Methodological Note on Facts and Valuations in Social Science," in *An American Dilemma*, *op. cit.*, pp. 1035-64.

4. Myrdal, *op. cit.*, pp. 1049-50.

5. E. B. Reuter, "Competition and the Racial Division of Labor," as quoted in Myrdal, *op. cit.*, p. 1051.

6. William F. Ogburn, "Man and His Institutions," as quoted in Myrdal, *op. cit.*, p. 1051.

7. Myrdal, *op. cit.*, p. 1051 n.

8. *Ibid.*, p. 1053.

9. *Ibid.*

10. *Ibid.*, pp. 1031-32.

11. *Ibid.*, p. 1056.

12. *Ibid.*

13. Ralph Ellison, *"An American Dilemma*: A Review," in *Shadow and Act* (New York, Random House, 1964), pp. 303-17.

14. Ellison, *op. cit.*, p. 313. Emphasis in original.

15. *Ibid.*, p. 313.

16. *Ibid.*, p. 314.

17. Myrdal, *op. cit.*, p. 1069. Emphasis in original.

18. *Ibid.*

19. *Cf.* Nahum Z. Medalia, "Myrdal's Assumptions on Race Relations: A Conceptual Commentary," *Social Forces*, 40 (March, 1962), pp. 223-37.

20. Myrdal, *op. cit.*, pp. 1062-63. Emphasis in original.

21. *Ibid.*, p. *xlviii.*

22. *Ibid.*, p. 3.

23. *Ibid.*, p. *xlvii.*

24. Winthrop D. Jordan, *White Over Black: American Attitudes Toward the Negro, 1550-1812* (Chapel Hill, University of North Carolina Press, 1968).

25. F. Scott Fitzgerald, *The Crack Up* (New York, New Directions, 1959), p. 69.

26. See *e.g.,* Donald T. Campbell and Robert A. LeVine, "Ethnocentrism and Intergroup Relations" in Robert P. Abelson *et al., Theories of Cognitive Consistency: A Sourcebook* (Chicago, Rand McNally, 1968), pp. 551-64.

27. Maurice Merleau-Ponty, "A Note on Machiavelli," *Signs*, trans. by Richard C. McCleary (Evanston, Ill., Northwestern University Press, 1964), pp. 211-23.

28. I have in mind here existentialist and phenomenological

philosophy. For its application to sociology see Edward A. Tiryakian, "Existential Phenomenology and Sociology," *American Sociological Review*, 30 (December, 1965), pp. 647-88.

29. See Stanford M. Lyman and Marvin B. Scott, *A Sociology of the Absurd* (New York, Appleton-Century-Crofts, 1970).
30. W. E. B. Du Bois, "The Negro Citizen," as quoted in Myrdal, *op. cit.*, p. 512.
31. Myrdal, *op. cit.*, pp. 513-18.
32. *Ibid.*, p. 518. Emphasis in original.
33. *Ibid.*, p. 519.
34. *Ibid.*
35. *Ibid.*, p. 520.
36. See *e.g.,* W. S. M. Banks III, "The Rank Order of Sensitivity to Discriminations of Negroes in Columbus, Ohio," *American Sociological Review*, 15 (August, 1950), pp. 529-34; E. E. Edmunds, "The Myrdalian Thesis: Rank Order of Discrimination," *Phylon*, 15 (1954), pp. 297-303; E. Q. Campbell, "Moral Discomfort and Race Segregation—An Examination of the Myrdal Hypothesis," *Social Forces*, 39 (March, 1961), pp. 228-34; and L. M. Killian and C. M. Grigg, "Rank Orders of Discrimination and Negroes and Whites in a Southern City," *Social Forces*, 39 (March, 1961), pp. 235-39.
37. Myrdal, *op. cit.*, p. 61.
38. *Ibid.*, p. li.
39. Ellison, *op. cit.*, pp. 315-16.
40. Myrdal, *op. cit.*, pp. 643-44 *et passim*.
41. *Ibid.*, pp. 1073-78.
42. *Ibid.*, p. liii.
43. *Ibid.*
44. Robert S. Lynd, *Knowledge for What?* (New York, Grove Press, 1964), pp. 202-50.

CHAPTER V

Psychological Theories of Race Prejudice:
The Black as a Victim of a White Personality Disorder

1. Gordon Allport, "Prejudice: A Problem in Psychological and Social Causation," in *Toward a General Theory of Action: Theoretical Foundations for the Social Sciences* (New York, Harper Torchbooks, 1962), p. 366.
2. *Ibid.*, p. 365.
3. Allport, *The Nature of Prejudice*, abr. ed. (Garden City, N.Y., Doubleday Anchor, 1958), p. 398
4. *Ibid.*, p. 401.
5. *Ibid.*, p. 410.
6. *Ibid.*, p. 8.
7. In sociological thought there has been a persistent movement toward "normalizing" what the psychologists have called "rationalizations." See Gresham M. Sykes and David Matza, "Techniques of Neutralization: A Theory of Delinquency," *American Sociological Review*, 22 (December, 1957), pp. 664-70; Marvin B. Scott and Stanford M. Lyman, "Accounts," *American Sociological Review*, 33 (February, 1968), pp. 46-62; and Erving Goffman, "The Insanity of Place," *Psychiatry*, 32 (November, 1969), esp. pp. 365-67.
8. Allport, *The Nature of Prejudice*, op. cit., pp. 320-21.
9. T. W. Adorno, Else Frenkel-Brunswick, Daniel J. Levinson, and R. Nevitt Sanford, *The Authoritarian Personality* (New York, Harper and Row, 1950).
10. Allport, *The Nature of Prejudice*, op. cit., p. 383.
11. *Ibid.*, p. 212.
12. Allport, "Prejudice: Is It Societal or Personal?" *The Person in Psychology: Selected Essays of Gordon W. Allport* (Boston, Beacon Press, 1968), p. 191.
13. Allport, *The Nature of Prejudice*, op. cit., pp. 271-81.
14. Allport, "Prejudice and the Individual," in *The American Negro Reference Book*, John P. Davis, ed. (Englewood Cliffs, N.J., Prentice-Hall, 1966), p. 712.
15. Allport does suggest a pattern of neurotic conformity exemplified by the behavior and statements of Rudolph Hoess, com-

mandant at Auschwitz, who carried out the murder of 2,500,000 persons without ever thinking about the morality of his actions. Allport concludes on this point: "We can only learn from this case that a fanatic ideology may engender conformity of incredible tenacity."—Allport, *The Nature of Prejudice*, *op. cit.*, p. 275.

16. Allport, "Prejudice and the Individual," *op. cit.*, p. 708.
17. Allport, *The Nature of Prejudice*, *op. cit.*, pp. 283-84.
18. *Ibid.*, p. 285.
19. *Ibid.*, p. 284.
20. See Benjamin B. Wolman, *Contemporary Theories and Systems in Psychology* (New York, Harper and Row, 1960), p. 418.
21. Allport, *Nature of Prejudice*, *op. cit.*, pp. 287-89.
22. *Ibid.*, p. 295.
23. *Ibid.*, p. 452.
24. *Ibid.*, p. 456.
25. *Ibid.*
26. *Ibid.*, p. 459.
27. *Ibid.*
28. *Ibid.*, p. 461.
29. *Ibid.*, p. 460.
30. *Ibid.*, pp. 383-84.
31. Allport, "Prejudice and the Individual," *op. cit.*, p. 707.
32. See, *e.g.*, Reinhard Bendix, "Compliant Behavior and Individual Personality," *American Journal of Sociology*, 58 (November, 1952), pp. 292-303.
33. Many of Allport's later essays have a fairly strong polemical tone and are written in reply to his critics. See, for example, "Prejudice: Is It Societal or Personal?" *op. cit.*, and the sources cited therein.
34. The critical literature on *The Authoritarian Personality* is too voluminous to list here. For a bibliography up to 1956 see Richard Christie and Peggy Cook, "A Guide to Published Literature Relating to the Authoritarian Personality Through 1956," *Journal of Psychology*, 45 (1958), pp. 171-91. The most significant criticism is perhaps Richard Christie and Marie Jahoda, *Studies in the Scope and Method of "The Authoritarian Personality"* (Glencoe, Ill., Free Press, 1954).

For a comprehensive and up-to-date critique see Roger Brown, *Social Psychology* (New York, Free Press, 1965), pp. 477-546. See also William Petersen, "Prejudice in American Society: A Critique of Some Recent Formulations," *Commentary*, 26 (October, 1958), pp. 342-48.

35. Herbert Blumer, "Race Prejudice As a Sense of Group Position," *Pacific Sociological Review*, I (Spring, 1958), pp. 3-7. All quotations are from this essay unless otherwise specified.

CHAPTER VI

The Social System and the Black American:
The Sociological Perspective of Talcott Parsons

1. Talcott Parsons, "Certain Primary Sources and Patterns of Aggression in the Social Structure of the Western World," *Essays in Sociological Theory* (New York, Free Press, 1964), pp. 298-322.
2. *Ibid.*, p. 304.
3. *Ibid.*, p. 306.
4. *Ibid.*, p. 307.
5. *Ibid.*, pp. 308-19.
6. Norman Mailer, *The White Negro* (San Francisco, City Lights Books, 1957).
7. Parsons, *op. cit.*, p. 313.
8. *Ibid.*, p. 310.
9. *Ibid.*, p. 318.
10. The most recent instance of this charge is found in Tom Bottomore, "Out of This World," *New York Review of Books*, XIII (November 6, 1969), pp. 34-39. See also Max Black, ed., *The Social Theories of Talcott Parsons: A Critical Examination* (Englewood Cliffs, N.J., Prentice-Hall, 1961); and Ralf Dahrendorf, "Out of Utopia: Toward a Reorientation of Sociological Analysis," *Essays in the Theory of Society* (Stanford, Calif., Stanford University Press, 1968), pp. 107-28.
11. Parsons, "Full Citizenship for the Negro American? A Sociological Problem," in Talcott Parsons and Kenneth B. Clark,

eds., *The Negro American* (Boston, Houghton Mifflin, 1966), pp. 709-54.

12. *Ibid.*, p. 717.
13. *Ibid.*, p. 718.
14. *Ibid.*
15. *Ibid.*, p. 719.
16. *Ibid.*
17. Parsons adapts this phrase from Seymour Martin Lipset, *The First New Nation: The United States in Historical and Comparative Perspective* (New York, Basic Books, 1963).
18. Parsons, "Full Citizenship for the Negro American? A Sociological Problem," *op. cit.*, p. 721.
19. *Ibid.*, pp. 738-39.
20. Parsons, "Introduction: Why 'Freedom Now,' Not Yesterday?" in Parsons and Clark, *op. cit.*, p. *xxiii*.
21. *Ibid.*, p. *xxiv*.
22. See Parsons, *Societies: Evolutionary and Comparative Perspectives* (Englewood Cliffs, N.J., Prentice-Hall, 1966).
23. Parsons, "Full Citizenship for the Negro American?" *op. cit.*, p. 744.
24. *Ibid.*, p. 750.
25. Parsons, "Introduction: Why 'Freedom Now,' Not Yesterday?" *op. cit.*, pp. *xxvii-xxviii*.

CHAPTER VII

Toward a Sociology of the Black in America

1. Frederick Teggart, *The Theory and Processes of History* (Berkeley, University of California Press, 1941), p. 244.
2. Margaret T. Hodgen, *Change and History: A Study of the Dated Distributions of Technological Innovations in England*, (Viking Fund Publications in Anthropology, No. 18; New York, Wenner-Gren Foundation for Anthropological Research, 1952).
3. Kenneth E. Bock, *The Acceptance of Histories: Toward a Perspective for Social Science* (University of California

Publications in Sociology and Social Institutions, Vol. III, No. 1; Berkeley, University of California Press, 1956), p. 112.

4. *Ibid.*, pp. 114-15.

5. *Ibid.*, p. 115.

6. Robert A. Nisbet, *Social Change and History* (New York, Oxford University Press, 1969), pp. 270-304.

7. See Harold Garfinkel, *Studies in Ethnomethodology* (Englewood Cliffs, N.J., Prentice-Hall, 1968).

8. W. I. Thomas, *Source Book for Social Origins* (Boston, Richard G. Badger, 1909), p. 17.

9. Nisbet, *op. cit.*, p. 277.

10. For this concept see Alfred Schutz, "Some Structures of the Life World," in I. Schutz, ed., *Collected Papers III: Studies in Phenomenological Philosophy* (The Hague, Martinus Nijhoff, 1966), pp. 116-32.

11. See *e.g.,* Paul Edwards, ed., *Equiano's Travels: The Interesting Narrative of the Life of Olaudah Equiano, or Gustavus Vassa the African* (New York, Frederick A. Praeger, 1966), pp. 1-30. First published in 1789.

12. See, *e.g.,* M. R. Delany and Robert Campbell, *Search for a Place: Black Separatism and Africa, 1860* (Ann Arbor, University of Michigan Press, 1969); William E. Bittle and Gilbert Geis, *The Longest Way Home: Chief Alfred C. Sam's Back-to-Africa Movement* (Detroit, Wayne State University Press, 1964), Edwin S. Redkey, *Black Exodus: Black Nationalist and Back-to-Africa Movements, 1890-1910* (New Haven, Conn., Yale University Press, 1969); Amy Jacques Garvey, comp., *The Philosophy and Opinions of Marcus Garvey, or Africa for the Africans* (London, Frank Cass, 1967); and Edmund David Cronon, *Black Moses: The Story of Marcus Garvey and the Universal Negro Improvement Association* (Madison, Unviersity of Wisconsin Press, 1964).

13. See St. Clair Drake, "Hide My Face—On Pan Africanism and Negritude," in Herbert Hill, ed., *Soon, One Morning: New Writing by American Negroes, 1940-1962* (New York, Alfred A. Knopf, 1963), pp. 77-105; the papers by Saunders Redding, Samuel W. Allen, John Henrik Clarke, Julian Mayfield, and Arthur P. Davis in *The The American Negro Writer and*

His Roots: Selected Papers from the First Conference of Negro Writers (New York, American Society of African Culture, 1960); and Jaja A. Wachuku, "The Relationship of AMSAC and the American Negro to Africa and Pan-Africanism," in *Pan-Africanism Reconsidered*, edited by the American Society of African Culture (AMSAC) (Berkeley, University of California Press, 1962).

14. See E. U. Essien-Udom, *Black Nationalism: A Search for an Identity in America* (Chicago, University of Chicago Press, 1962); Archie Epps, ed., *The Speeches of Malcolm X at Harvard* (New York, William Morrow, 1968); and Floyd B. Barbour, ed., *The Black Power Revolt* (Boston, Extending Horizon Books—Porter Sargent, 1968).

15. See Harold Cruse, *The Crisis of the Negro Intellectual from Its Origins to the Present* (New York, William Morrow, 1967), and *Rebellion or Revolution* (New York, William Morrow, 1968).

16. For the conception employed here see Maurice Merleau-Ponty, "A Note on Machiavelli," *Signs*, trans. by Richard C. McCleary (Evanston, Ill., Northwestern University Press, 1964), pp. 211-23; and Stanford M. Lyman and Marvin B. Scott, *A Sociology of the Absurd* (New York, Appleton-Century-Crofts, 1970), Chap. I.

17. Thomas, *op. cit.*, pp. 18-19.

18. See Lyman and Scott, *op. cit.* For the philosophy of the absurd see Albert Camus, *The Myth of Sisyphus and Other Essays*, trans. by Justin O'Brien (New York, Vintage Books, 1955); for the dramatics of the absurd see Martin Esslin, *The Theatre of the Absurd* (Garden City, N.Y., Doubleday Anchor Books, 1969).

19. Quoted in Esslin, *op. cit.*, p. 5.

20. For these concepts see Alfred Schutz, *The Phenomenology of the Social World*, trans. by George Walsh and Frederick Lehnert, (Evanston, Ill., Northwestern University Press, 1967), pp. 163-214.

21. Quoted in Richard Hofstadter, *The Progressive Historians: Turner, Beard, Parrington* (New York, Alfred A. Knopf, 1969), p. 3.

Index

Index

A